Celebrating Nature

Celebrating Nature

Rites and Ceremonies Around the World

by ELIZABETH S. HELFMAN

drawings by Carolyn Cather

THE SEABURY PRESS • NEW YORK

LIBRARY OF CONGRESS CATALOG CARD NUMBER: 73-79943

Design by Carol Basen
Printed in the United States of America

Acknowledgments

I wish to thank the following publishers and authors for permission to use copyrighted material from the titles listed:

Ernest Benn Limited for two verses from *The Gods of Mexico* by Lewis Spence, published by T. Fisher Unwin, 1923.

Robert Brittain for part of an Egyptian prayer quoted in his book, *Rivers, Man, and Myths.*

The Clarendon Press, Oxford, for the first four lines of "Round and Round the Maypole" from *The Lore and Language of Schoolchildren* by Iona and Peter Opie.

Thomas Y. Crowell Company for six lines of verse from *The Book of Holidays* by J. Walker McSpadden.

Doubleday & Company for two lines of verse from *Six Thousand Years of Bread* by H. E. Jacob. Copyright 1944 by H. E. Jacob.

Epworth Press for a verse from *West African Religion* by Geoffrey Parrinder.

Oxford University Press, Bombay, for the Saora ikon and prayer from *The Religion of an Indian Tribe* by Verrier Elwin.

Oxford University Press, London, for a verse from *Religion and Medicine of the Ga People* by M. J. Field.

Oxford University Press, New York, for three lines of Gerard Manley Hopkins' poem, "Hurrahing in Harvest," from *Poems of Gerard Manley Hopkins,* edited by Robert Bridges.

Random House, Inc., for a quotation from *Facing Mount Kenya* by Jomo Kenyatta.

Routledge & Kegan Paul Ltd. for four lines of verse from *People of the Small Arrow* by J. H. Driberg.

The World Publishing Company for three lines of a song from *The Ancient Sun Kingdoms of the Americas* by Victor Von Hagen.

Contents

TO HELEN GRIFFITH

part I

In Earliest Times

Prelude

IN SILENCE, SINGLE FILE, A SMALL GROUP of dark-skinned men slowly climb steep rocks to reach a cave in the wall of a ravine. On the face of the rock in the cave are sacred drawings, made by the ancestors of these men ages ago. There is a semicircle of small stones on the floor of the cave, placed there just as long ago. Standing by these stones, the men sing songs that are a part of an ancient rite of their tribe. Bending rhythmically, as in a dance, they strike the stones with special twigs they have brought. This, too, is a part of the rite.

These men are members of the Witchetty Grub Clan, part of the Arunta tribe in Central Australia. They live on a vast desert where only scrub and a few trees can survive throughout the year. Rain comes seldom, but when it does come it pours down in torrents, and suddenly the desert blossoms as the rose. Plants, flowers, birds, insects, and other wildlife appear as if by magic. It seems to these people of the desert that this sudden upsurge of life has been sent by the spirits who created life everywhere on earth. It is spirits, too, who send the witchetty grub, a food so special that this clan was named for it.

The Witchetty Grub people and their neighbors of other clans live by hunting animals and insects and gathering wild fruits and seeds. They believe that if they do not perform the ancient rites the spirits will not send an abundance of food. The people may starve. These rites are religious ceremonies performed in a set pattern, at special times of the year, for the gods or spirits who control man's world.

Each year when the rains are due, men of the Witchetty

Grub Clan climb to their cave in the wall of a ravine. There they perform a ceremony designed to increase the supply of the insects, for the benefit of all the people. Their ancestors faithfully performed this same ceremony, probably for thousands of years.

The circle of stones in the cave represents the witchetty grub and its eggs. The men hope that there will be many eggs this year. When they have finished their ritual around the stones they start back to camp. On the way they pause to decorate themselves with sacred designs of the witchetty grub and with feathers and twigs.

At the camp, they wriggle into a long narrow hut built of branches, representing the chrysalis from which the witchetty grub emerges. There they sing of the insect in the various stages of its growth, from egg to grub to chrysalis and then the beetle itself. They sing, too, of the sacred stones they visited in the cave. They are hungry and thirsty; food and water are brought to them.

At dusk the men shuffle out of the hut, as the insect comes out of its chrysalis. Still singing about the witchetty grub, they sit around a blazing fire until daybreak. Surely the spirits have watched and listened to their ceremony. There will be enough to eat for everyone, and not just witchetty grubs. The Undiara Kangaroo Clan performs ceremonies each year to increase the supply of kangaroo meat. Other foods will be plentiful because other clans perform their own rites to assure the supply of food for all the people.

These dark-skinned Australians of the desert live much

as hunting people did in the Stone Age, about ten thousand years ago, using only tools made of stone or bone. Their rites may be much the same as those of hunters in very early times, in other parts of the world.

I

Man on the Earth

THE WORLD OF STONE AGE MAN WAS FULL OF DANGER AND uncertainty. Fierce animals roamed the woods. Hunger came often; so, too, did death and disease. Early people needed all of their sharp wits to stay alive in this world, but they did not rely only on their wits. It seemed to them that there were spirits in all the world around them. Everything that happened was controlled by spirits and they controlled man, too. Spirits were more powerful than he could ever dream of being.

Early man was never sure what these spirits would do. They might black out the sun in the sky, making perpetual night. They might withhold the good rain that brought water to the earth. Then the green plants in the earth could not grow, and sickness and death would descend upon the people. Men felt they must try to please the spirits, so that day would follow night and life would flourish on the earth.

Compared with what we know about people who lived

in later times, we know very little about these people of long ago. They had no written language. The little we do know comes mainly from a study of paintings and sculpture and carvings they made, and tools they left behind—fishhooks, spears, hatchets, bows and arrows, scrapers, and carving tools.

Anthropologists have learned about them, too, by studying the customs of very primitive people who are living on earth today, such as the Aruntas of the Australian desert. Like the Aruntas, the earliest people in the world were hunters and food gatherers. They gathered berries and fruits that grew wild nearby, and they hunted wild animals so they could eat their flesh.

Hunting was a hazardous business for early man. Big animals could hunt *him,* too. He had to try to make sure that when he went out to hunt, the aim of his spear or his arrow would be true and he would bring an animal back to the camp. It would never do to leave this to chance, or even to his own skill—skillful though he was. He must perform certain rites, so the spirits who controlled the animal world would help him.

Early man did not pray in words to these spirits. He did not sit and think about what to do. This was not his way. Instead, he *acted.* He needed to feel in his own body the magic that was to influence the spirits.

Deep inside of caves, by the light of torches, early man painted pictures of the animals he wanted to kill. He painted bison, or a herd of reindeer, a wild pig running or a wolf jumping. Some of the animals he painted had been speared in the heart and were dying.

Since early man used action to express his feelings about

the world, he must have acted out the hunt, deep in his cave. Over and over again he would throw his spear at the heart of the animal in the painting, just as he hoped to do in the hunt. Lifting the spear, aiming it, throwing it—this became a kind of dance, and the dance was a kind of magic. If he could spear the animal in the cave, he thought, the spirits of the wild would help him to spear it when he went into the woods.

This dance probably had several meanings for early man. It helped him in the hunt, but it must have done more than that. It may have helped him to forget, even if only for a little while, the fear that went with him as he

Cave painting

walked through the woods, a victim of storm, wind, and cold, and of the wild animals he hunted. Early man probably felt like a new person after his dance, as if he were in touch with powers beyond himself.

People knew that good hunting was impossible unless there were plenty of animals. So it was wise to make sure that these animals, and the fish in the streams too, reproduced their kind. Ritual could help with this as well as with the hunt. Paintings in the caves showed male and female animals together, with their young. Ritual dances reminded the spirits that it was important for young life to be brought into the world—not only young animals, but the children of man, too.

For these early people the dark places in caves where they made pictures and danced their ritual were sanctuaries, sacred places where they communicated with the spirits who controlled their lives.

All of these people lived very close to the earth. In fear and wonder they performed rites for the spirits who inhabited the world around them—hoping, if only for a little while, to live in peace.

Somewhere between six thousand and seven thousand years ago, people learned to plant seeds and grow their own food in their own gardens. They no longer lived only by hunting animals and gathering fruits and grains that grew wild. People kept on hunting, too, for this was a way of getting a variety of food and there was excitement in the hunt. But gardens gradually became more and more important in their lives.

People had always been aware of the changing seasons.

Those who lived where the winters were cold saw the green plants on earth wither and seem to die each winter. Every year this winter came and every year it was new and terrible —a long hard time, often bringing hunger. The earliest people did not even have the comfort of knowing that spring would surely come again to warm the earth so the green leaves could grow and the flowers bloom.

The seasons had a new meaning for people when they learned to plant seeds of the wild grain and other plants that grew on the hillsides. They had known for a long time that seeds were good to eat. Planting them was another matter. The earth was scratched with digging sticks when the sun had warmed it in the spring. Seeds were planted in the furrows. The grain grew tall under the summer sun, and in late summer or fall it was ready for reaping. This was the good pattern of the seasons, year after year, all of it controlled by the spirits who ruled the earth. It was the pattern of man's life, too.

At first it was the women who sowed the seeds in the earth, and the earth itself was considered the Great Mother of all life. With a feeling of fear and guilt people begged for forgiveness when they hurt the earth by scratching it to make a place for the seeds. Gifts were given to the Earth Mother and each year part of the harvest was offered to her. All of it belonged to her, but since the people must live too, part of the harvest symbolized the whole.

Rituals in drama and dance were performed when the seeds were sown, and again when the grain was reaped. It was important to please not only the Earth Mother but all the spirits of the natural world. There was much that was good in this world—life and growth and food to eat. But often there was evil, too—death and disease and hunger. If the right rituals were performed and the spirits were pleased, then surely spring would follow winter, the grain would ripen, and good would overcome evil. This was a part of the religion of man in early times.

Like the earlier people who were hunters, these people needed to feel in their own bodies their prayer to the spirits, their thanks to the Earth Mother. They acted out the growth of the grain in the summer, and the drama of the death of vegetation in the winter and its rebirth in the spring. That way the spirits of all growing things would know that man depended on them to continue the pattern of life on the earth. Without this feeling for a world of spirits beyond himself, early man was convinced he could not live.

The planting of grain and other plants brought about great changes in the lives of early people. Seeds could be planted near the home cave or hut. As long as there was enough rain, people could live beside their gardens instead of wandering in search of game. For the first time, groups of people settled in villages.

These changes occurred slowly, over many years, in the period of history we call the New Stone Age. There were then people living in every habitable part of the world. Not many people, compared with those on earth today, but little groups here and there.

Of course, the pattern of the seasons was not the same everywhere. Where winters were cold, grain was planted in the spring. Where winters were cool, or even fairly warm, grain might be planted in the fall and grow through the winter. Then the reaping would come in the spring. The kind of ritual people performed, and the time of year, depended on the climate, the land, and man's own inclinations. But whatever the differences, the pattern of seedtime and harvest meant life itself.

This pattern of the seasons, from spring to winter, from seedtime to harvest, has played an important part in the lives of men all through the centuries. People felt they had to make sure that this life-giving pattern would not fail. For this purpose they devised different rites and ceremonies, dedicated to their different gods.

For thousands of years the growing of plants for food was itself considered a religious act. So was man's welcoming of the springtime, and all his rites and ceremonies marking the seasons. Gradually this changed, until most celebrations and festivals were no longer concerned primarily with the growth of plants for food, or with the seasons, or even with nature at all.

This book is about rites and ceremonies that *did* celebrate the earth and everything that grows upon it, and all the seasons of the year. (We often use the words rite and ceremony interchangeably. Both have a religious meaning in this book, but strictly speaking, *rite* refers to the precise form a ceremony takes. The ceremony is an act performed by custom which has a meaning beyond its outward appearance.) Many of these ceremonies belong to the past; some are still performed today. A number of important religious ceremonies are not included in this book because they do not fit this pattern.

Though our celebrations have changed, people today are as much a part of nature as they have ever been. You may have already felt this if you have watched plants grow in the fields through the summer and bear fruit in the earth.

But what can all this have to do with you if you live in the city, in a tall building between other tall buildings? A great deal, after all. You are no less a part of nature. Look up at the moon in the night sky. Feel the sun and the rain on your face. Along your street or in a park, watch the tight pink buds on the trees uncurl into leaves in the spring. In summer, as you walk beneath the trees, look up into a green world of leaves. Sniff the air in autumn when there has been a touch of frost. Watch the leaves that have fallen from the trees as they scatter in the wind. The natural world is forever changing, even in the city. Seasons belong to you, too.

2

The Ancient Egyptians

THE PERIOD OF HISTORY WHICH WE CALL ANCIENT BEGAN almost six thousand years ago and lasted for more than four thousand years. This seems very long ago to us, but it was many thousands of years after early man painted his pictures of animals in the dark caves.

As time went on, certain patterns developed in the beliefs and rituals connected with the seasons, with seedtime and harvest, in various parts of the world. Myths were told. These were elaborate stories of the lives and adventures of the gods and goddesses who controlled the natural world.

The Earth Mother was worshiped everywhere. She was honored when the seed was put into the earth. At harvest, when the soil was exhausted from the growth of the grain, there were dances to please the Earth Mother, so that she would renew the earth. Sometimes a human being was sacrificed, killed and given to the earth, to ensure fertility. Life was given for the sake of life to be. Later, animals were sacrificed instead.

People came to believe, in time, that the Earth Mother was not the sole source of life on earth. There was also the Sky Father, who sent the rain without which nothing could grow. Both were honored with ritual and dance. In some places the Earth Mother continued to be of first importance. In other places the Sky Father took her place.

The earliest civilizations began in the valleys of great rivers, the Nile in Africa and the Tigris and Euphrates in Asia Minor. The harvest of grain was abundant in these valleys. People could grow more than just enough food for themselves. Some of the people had time for singing and dancing, time to paint pictures, to write on sheets of papyrus or on clay tablets, to cut words in stone or carve beautiful statues. Others were slaves, busy with little more than the grim business of keeping themselves and other people alive.

Villages beside the fields of grain grew into towns, towns into cities. Civilization meant more people living together. Rites and ceremonies were no longer always performed by small groups of people. Often crowds took part.

In ancient Egypt the growth of the grain depended on the yearly flooding of the Nile River. Then as now, this was a land where it seldom rained. Without the river Egypt would be a desert. Each summer torrential rains fell in the mountains far to the south. Tons of swirling water flowed down the river into Egypt and spread out over its broad valley. Then slowly, as the water became less abundant, it retreated into the river again. Some of the water remained in man-made canals that crossed the fields.

The seasonal rituals and celebrations of the Egyptians followed the pattern of the river. Feasts were held for twenty-four days each year when the flood waters were first pouring down the river. All the people took part in the feasts. They had time to celebrate; no work could be done in the fields while they were flooded. This was the Egyptian New Year.

As the waters of the Nile poured down, offerings were made to Hapi, god of the river, while the people sang:

Offerings are made to thee,
Oxen are slain to thee,
Great festivals are kept for thee,
Pure flames are offered to thee.

The grain was sown in the fall, in the rich soil left on the muddy fields after the water had subsided. This was the time of festivals in honor of the god Osiris.

The whole story of Osiris is too long to tell here. There were, in fact, many tales, some of them contradictory. Osiris was said to have been a ruler of Egypt, with his queen-sister Isis. (All Egyptian rulers were supposed to be gods.) The evil brother of Osiris, Set, killed him, cut his body into pieces, and scattered the pieces from one end of Egypt to the other. Isis, however, found the pieces of Osiris' body and put them together, so that the god lived again.

Osiris was a very popular god with the Egyptians. He was associated with the sprouting of the grain that brought life to people on earth. To the Egyptians he remained the god of growing things even though after he was killed he became ruler of the underworld, where people went when they died. (Horus, son of Osiris, replaced his father here on earth as the young god of vegetation.)

Osiris meant more than the sprouting of the grain to

the Egyptians. He brought the whole renewal of nature each year, as did the rising waters of the Nile. Since he himself did not die, perhaps the people of Egypt, too, would go on living even after death. And their kings, the Pharaohs, would be born again each year.

The rites held at seedtime in honor of Osiris went on for many days. The pattern varied in different parts of Egypt. Everywhere, however, his death and resurrection

Figure of Osiris with sprouting grain

were acted out. Sometimes an image of the god was made. In one place a clay image was fashioned of earth mixed with grain and moistened with water from the Nile. The face of the image was painted yellow and the cheek bones green. Often the grain would sprout before the rites were finished. Then the likeness of the god would seem to be covered with soft green fur.

As the clay form of Osiris took shape the people would shout all up and down the river: "We have found him! We rejoice!"

The image of the god was taken in procession to the temple, where it was placed in a room that represented his tomb.

In one ceremony, after a plowing and sowing rite, the image of Osiris was floated on the river with other images of gods in thirty-four tiny boats lighted by 365 candles, one for each day of the year. Then, on the last day of the celebration, the effigy of the god was laid to rest in an underground chamber, to stay until the following year.

Isis was the Earth Mother in Egyptian religion. She was less important than her brother-husband, Osiris, though she had her part in the seasonal festivals. But the Egyptian farmer knew her worth. He knew that the ripe grain he cut down at harvest belonged to her. So he would pause after cutting the first few blades of grain, beat his breast loudly, and call on Isis to forgive him.

As we have seen, all the rites in honor of Osiris, varied though they were, portrayed his death, burial, and resurrec-

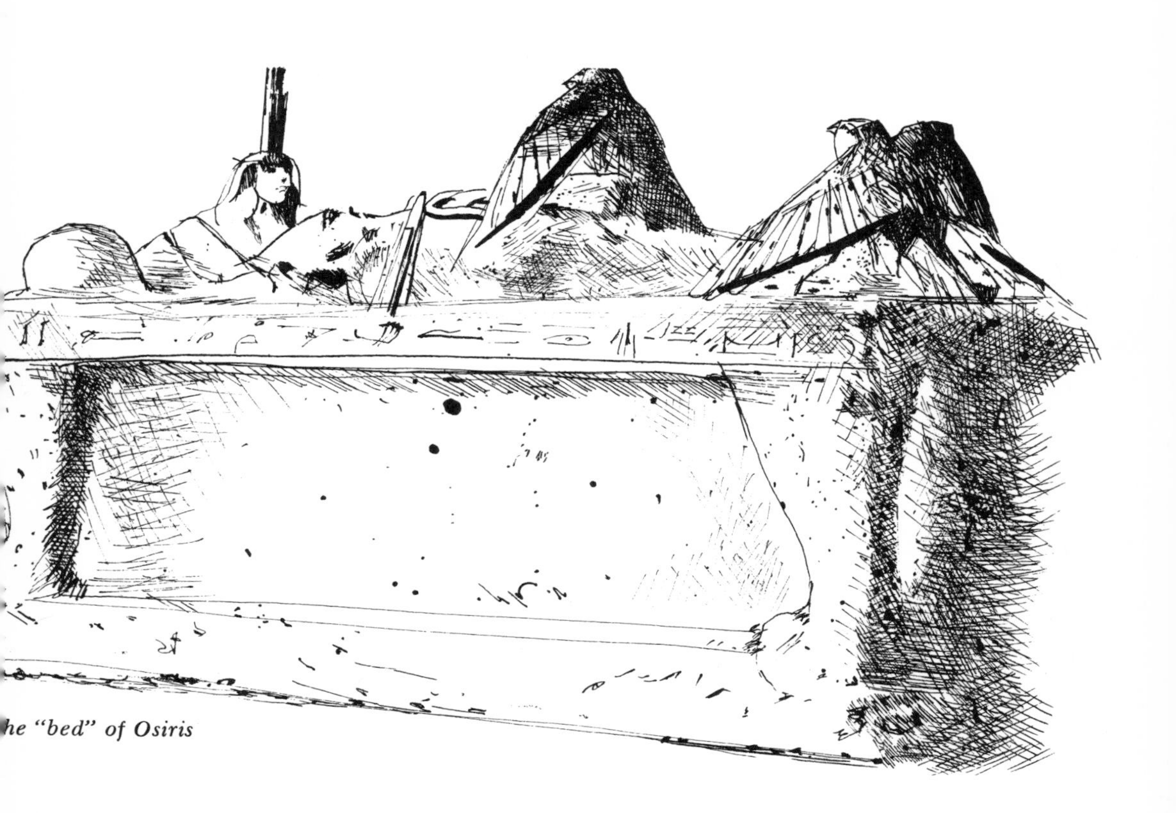

he "bed" of Osiris

tion. The death and rebirth of a god or a hero form a pattern which is found in many different religions, in different parts of the world.

In early times the rebirth of the god was a symbol of the green plants that appeared on the earth when the cold winter had gone, or, in warmer climates, when the seeds that had been planted sprouted and started to grow.

Harvest time in the warm climate of Egypt was in the spring. It was celebrated with a festival. Thanks were given to the god Min (a form of Horus, son of Osiris) who brought fertility to the earth. Thanks were given, also, to other gods and goddesses, so none would feel left out. The king himself, the Pharaoh, walked in procession to the temple, between a sacred bull and an image of the god Min. It was the Pharaoh who cut the first sheaf of grain, and since he was a god, the people believed that this act would surely bring a plentiful harvest.

The cycle of the year was complete. The river had brought water, seed had grown in the earth, and the harvest made certain the continuation of life on earth. For this the Egyptians gave thanks to Osiris and Isis and Min, to Ra, the god of the sun, creator of the world, and to all the other gods and goddesses.

3

In the Land Between the Rivers

NOT FAR FROM EGYPT, TO THE EAST ACROSS THE ARABIAN peninsula, was the land called Mesopotamia in ancient times. Here, in the valley of the Tigris and Euphrates rivers, lived the people called Sumerians, and later, the Babylonians.

Like the valley of the Nile River, Mesopotamia, the "land between the rivers," had little rain. It was water from the rivers that kept this land from becoming a desert. An elaborate network of canals, dug by the people and kept in good condition year after year, carried the water of the rivers to the fields. The growth of the grain and the fruits of the land depended on the water in these canals.

The seasonal pattern in Mesopotamia was different from that in the Nile Valley. In Mesopotamia, in the spring and fall, rain sometimes poured down in torrents. Then the rivers might flood the land on either side of their banks. Sometimes whole villages were swept away. At other seasons there would be much less water in the rivers. The people could not depend on a single massive flood each year, as in Egypt.

Summer was long and hot; scorching winds blew across the dry land. Nothing could grow in the sun-baked soil. Then, with the fall rains, the earth came to life again. Wheat and barley and other grains were planted in the damp earth. Another crop was planted after the spring rains. Each time the growth of grain in the earth seemed a miracle.

Myths were told of the gods and goddesses who were thought to control this growth of the grain. As in Egypt, rituals were performed to ensure a good harvest from the land. In Mesopotamia a New Year's Festival was held when the long hot summer was over and the autumn rains came. Or, New Year might be celebrated, instead, when winter ended with the coming of rain in the spring. In early times, both New Years were celebrated in some places, because twice during the year the earth came to life with fruits and grain.

As in Egypt, a myth of the death and rebirth of a vegetation god was accompanied by ritual designed to help bring life back to earth. Here the god was Tammuz, and his name meant "true son of the deep water."

Tammuz was the young son and lover of Ishtar, the Earth Mother of Mesopotamia, source of all life. Tammuz the beautiful was swept away in a flood and descended to the land of darkness and death beneath the earth. Ishtar was desolate without him. She wandered through the dry cheerless fields of summer and at last she went down to the underworld in search of him. While Tammuz was away there was no increase in the life on earth. No grain could grow, no fruits could ripen. It seemed as if life might soon be gone from earth forever. Then a messenger was sent by Ea, the god of water, to bring Ishtar and Tammuz back to the earth. The queen of the underworld reluctantly allowed Ishtar to be sprinkled with the water of life. Tammuz was awakened from the sleep of death, and together they returned to the upper world. Green grain sprouted again on the earth, lambs were born, and life continued as it had since time began.

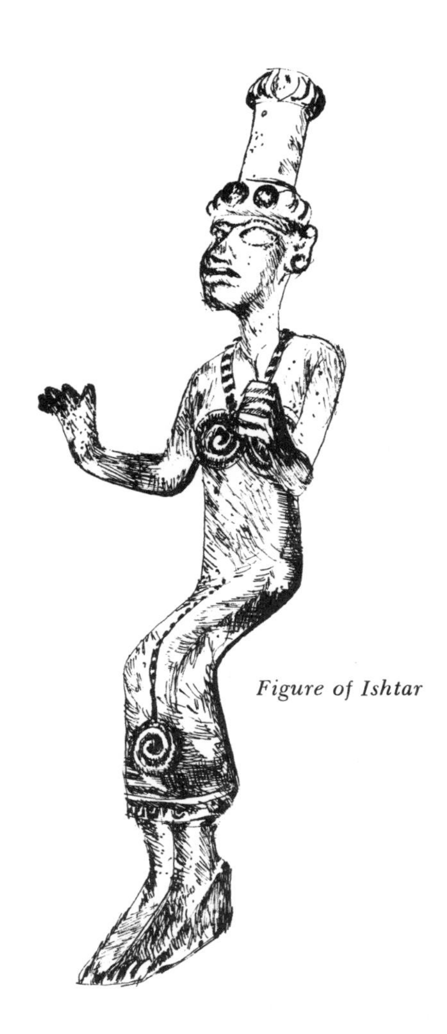

Figure of Ishtar

Every year, however, the drama was repeated. Tammuz had to spend half the year in the land of the dead, Ishtar pursued him there, and at last they returned to the upper world, bringing life with them.

The death of Tammuz was mourned each year in midsummer. Dirges were sung to the shrill music of flutes:

> The wailing is for the great river; it brings the flood
> no more.
> The wailing is for the fields of men; the grain grows
> no more. . . .
> The wailing is for the meadows; the bounty of the
> garden, the *sihlu* plants grow not. . . .

Other laments for the dead Tammuz have come down to us. They were written by Babylonian scribes on clay tablets. The laments were sung over a wooden effigy of the dead god which was washed with pure water, anointed with oil, and clothed in a red robe while the fragrance of incense rose in the air. Then the fate of the young Tammuz was acted out as the effigy was thrown into the Tigris or the Euphrates, where the water could lap over it as it had when the god himself was drowned.

The laments continued, in the hope that the gods would return Tammuz to the upper world so life could begin again.

This story of the death and rebirth of a god was full of meaning for people in ancient times. The god was a part of the growing world people saw around them. They themselves were a part of it, too. They believed that the god did indeed die each year, descend to the underworld, and come to life again. If this did not happen, they thought life would not increase and flourish on the earth.

4

Greek Myth and Ritual

THE STORY OF THE REBIRTH OF A GOD WAS TOLD THROUGHOUT the ancient world. In Asia Minor this god's name was Adonis, or sometimes Attis. The Earth Mother was called Cybele. As in Mesopotamia, the death of the god was mourned with bitter wailing. Images of Adonis were thrown into the sea or into springs. The rebirth of the god in some places was celebrated the following day.

"Gardens of Adonis" were sometimes planted by the women. Shallow baskets or pots were filled with earth and then seeds of wheat, barley, lettuce, and even flowers were planted in them. In the hot sun the plants shot up rapidly. But their roots could not grow deep in the shallow pots, and they would soon wither. At the end of eight days the pots were thrown into the sea or into springs along with the images of the dead Adonis.

Adonis was also known in ancient Greece, farther west on the Mediterranean Sea. In the Greek myth he was a beautiful youth much loved by Aphrodite, the goddess of love. She rambled through woods and over hills with him while he went hunting. Over and over again she warned him to keep away from dangerous animals. But Adonis was a brave young man and he paid no attention to such warnings. One day he wounded a wild boar. The beast rushed at him and tore him apart with its sharp tusks. The beautiful Adonis was dead. In her grief, Aphrodite changed his blood into a scarlet flower, the anemone. Adonis descended to the underworld, but like Tammuz, he was at last permitted to spend half the year on earth.

Demeter

The myth of Adonis grew out of the earlier Tammuz story. But the Greeks also had a goddess of the growing grain, with her own story and her own rites.

Demeter was the Greek goddess of the cultivated earth, especially of the grain. She wore white robes and carried sheaves of wheat and poppies in her hands. Persephone was Demeter's lovely daughter. One day Persephone was gathering flowers in a bright meadow. Suddenly the earth opened and Pluto, dark god of the underworld, came out of the earth and carried off Persephone in his golden chariot. He wanted her for queen in his shadowy kingdom.

Sorrowing, Demeter searched for her daughter over land and sea. When she was told what had happened, she was filled with anger. She would not let any seed grow in the earth until her daughter was restored to her. If no seeds could sprout, there would be no harvest, and without a harvest mankind would soon die of hunger.

The people on earth were desperate. At last Zeus, the father of the gods, commanded Pluto to give up Persephone for eight months of the year. During the other four months she must live with Pluto in the underworld.

While Persephone was on earth, fruit grew heavy on trees and vines, grain ripened, flowers blossomed in the meadows. When she must go again to the underworld, every year, nothing could grow in the earth. Thus, it was not the goddess of grain herself who was reborn, but her daughter.

In southern Greece, as in Mesopotamia, the barren season was the hot summer. Not a green stalk could be seen in the fields. These were the months when Persephone had gone to live with Pluto. When she returned in the fall, rain fell and the grain could be sown. It grew all through the cool months of winter, until harvest time in May.

The Greek farmer prayed to Demeter when he dropped his seeds into the brown earth, and when he had reaped his harvest he offered to her the first armful of golden grain.

Eleusis was the city in Greece where Demeter was supposed to have gone during her long search for her daughter. At Eleusis in September of each year rites and ceremonies were held in Demeter's honor. People walked in procession from the city of Athens to Eleusis. The festival lasted for nine days, the length of time that Demeter had wandered over the earth searching for Persephone. Offerings were made to all the many gods, so none need feel neglected. There was dancing in the streets. On the last day water was poured from east to west from earthen jars. Water, too, meant life.

Those who were to perform the special rites for Demeter bathed in the sea and wandered up and down the shore, carrying torches, acting out the sorrowing mother's search for her daughter. Then, in the sanctuary of the goddess, they took part in rites which they had sworn to keep secret. The secret was well kept, for we really do not know what took place. Probably in some form the drama of death and rebirth was acted out.

To the people who danced in the streets of Eleusis the rites, secret though they were, meant that new life began again each year as the grain sprouted in the earth. They could feel this happening in themselves; it was as if they, too, were born again.

The Greeks had many gods and goddesses, not all of them connected with nature and the seasons. For the country people of Greece, however, the mountains and fields and forests were haunted by countless gods and spirits. Spirits dwelt in trees and stones, in rivers and wells. Country people held their own ceremonies for these spirits, giving them gifts so that the wildlife on earth would prosper and do no harm to man.

Gaia was the Greek goddess of the uncultivated earth. Artemis was goddess of all the wild things. The country people of Greece held dances and masquerades for these goddesses who meant so much to those who lived close to the earth. And people in many parts of the world today have not forgotten these spirits of the wild, though they may know them by different names.

The old myths and rites were an expression of man's feeling that he was a part of nature and that nothing was more important in his world. We no longer believe in gods and goddesses of earth and sky, sun and rain, but the ancient myths can still have meaning for us. They may serve to remind us that we, too, are a part of the natural world.

5

The Hebrews in Palestine

AT THE FAR EASTERN END OF THE MEDITERRANEAN SEA, IN the land called Palestine, the ancient Hebrews celebrated the changing seasons in their own way. These were rugged and independent people who settled in Palestine about three thousand years ago. They were the first people to worship only one God. Today their descendants are called Jews.

The ancestors of the ancient Hebrews were herdsmen, wandering with their flocks of sheep and cattle. When a great famine came to the land, many of them went to Egypt to find food and settled there. The Pharaoh of Egypt made slaves of the Hebrews. These people who had been accustomed to the freedom of a wandering life thus had to spend their days in hard work under cruel masters.

After many years, under the leadership of Moses, the Hebrews finally escaped from Egypt sometime in the thirteenth century before Christ. They wandered in the Arabian desert for forty years before reaching Palestine, their "promised land."

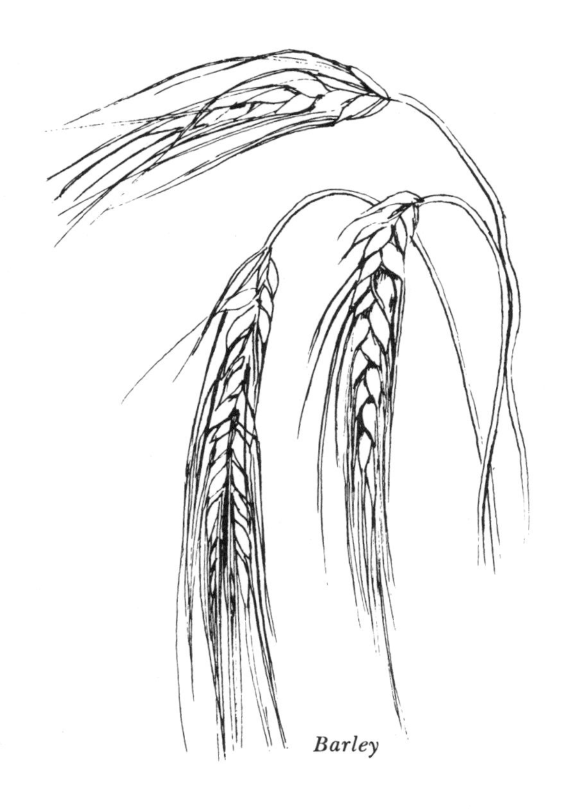

Barley

In Palestine the Hebrews became farming people. They settled in villages and planted their grain on the hillsides and in the valleys. There was seldom peace, because it took the Hebrews many years to drive out the Canaanites, who were already living in the valleys.

Except for the northern part, Palestine was a difficult land with a long rainless summer. But the Bible tells us that these wanderers from the desert found it "a good land, a land of brooks of water, of fountains and depths that spring out of valleys and hills; a land of wheat, and barley, and vines, and fig trees, and pomegranates; a land of oil olive, and honey. . . ." The dry summer of Palestine was not as lifeless as in Mesopotamia. Figs ripened on trees during this time, and grapes on the vine.

When the life-giving rains came at about the end of October, the dry land soaked up the water and all the pastures were green again. The earth was plowed and planted with grain on sunny days in February. Spring came in April, with bright flowers on the hillsides and green fields of grain in the valleys.

The Psalmist of the Bible wrote of this springtime: "The little hills rejoice on every side. The pastures are clothed with flocks; the valleys are covered with corn; they shout for joy, they also sing." (Corn meant any grain.)

Spring in Palestine was a season worth celebrating. The spring festival which the Jews call Passover was originally a combination of two rites of the ancient Hebrews. The early Hebrew herdsmen had sacrificed a lamb each spring to their god of fertility, giving back to the god a little of what he had given them. The Hebrew farmers celebrated the beginning of their spring barley harvest with a feast during which, for a week, only unleavened bread could be eaten. (Unleavened bread has no yeast or other substance to make it rise.) A sheaf of grain, gathered just before this first harvest, was brought to the priest in the Temple. "The first of the first fruits of thy land," says the Bible, "thou shalt bring into the house of the Lord thy God."

Since the sacrifice of the lamb and the feast for the first barley harvest took place in the same season, they were combined when the Hebrews began to worship one God. It was important to hold rites to assure the continuance of both the flocks on the hillside and the grain in the valleys.

The exodus from Egypt had also taken place at this season. In time, the spring festival of the Hebrews came to be mainly a celebration of this great liberation.

The Passover ritual of today still includes a prayer for dew, which was an important source of life-giving water in Palestine. These words from the Song of Solomon in the Bible are also read in the Passover service: "For lo, the winter is past, the rain is over and gone; the flowers appear on the earth; the time of the singing of birds is come, and the voice of the turtle [dove] is heard in our land."

Today, too, unleavened bread, called matzoth, is eaten during the week of Passover. It is supposed to represent the unleavened dough which the Hebrews in their haste took with them on their flight from Egypt.

The head of each family, at a gathering of children and guests on the first night of Passover, gives the answer to the ancient question, "How does this night differ from all other nights?" The deliverance from oppression in Egypt is celebrated together with the rebirth of the earth in spring.

Seven weeks after Passover, in our month of June, came a two-day festival, Shavuoth, the Feast of Weeks. Later this festival was also called Pentecost, from the Greek word for fifty, since it began fifty days after the beginning of Passover.

Shavuoth took place at the end of the spring wheat harvest. Pilgrims climbed the hill to the Temple, carrying a sheaf of new wheat. This was offered to God as the first fruits of the harvest. Two loaves of bread, baked with flour made from the new grain, were also brought.

Still other foods from the earth were carried to the Temple. "How blessed," sang the people, "are we to whom has been given this full harvest."

Later Shavuoth became a celebration of the day on which Moses received from God the Ten Commandments which were to be the Law of the Hebrew people.

Shavuoth is a happy holiday in the modern state of Israel. Streets are decorated with flowers and green boughs. Young people parade. Everyone sings and dances. In one harvest dance, couples move rhythmically as the reapers do when they cut grain. The man of each couple is the farmer; he swings his lady back and forth like a scythe.

In the fall, at the time of the grape harvest, the Hebrews celebrated another festival, Sukkoth, the Feast of Ingathering. There were seven days of this festival, each with its own ceremony. On each of the seven days pilgrims marched around the altar singing hymns and waving palm branches. There were torch dances at night.

Sukkoth was a thanksgiving festival for the harvest already given, and an expression of hope for the harvest to come. There were prayers to God for the rain that was so much needed after the dry summer.

Another name for this festival is the Feast of Tabernacles, or Booths. At this time little booths (called tabernacles or succahs) were made from the branches of trees, and set up on the roofs of houses, in courtyards, and other places. In the Bible, Nehemiah gave instructions for building these booths: "Go forth unto the mount, and fetch olive branches, and pine branches, and myrtle branches, and palm branches, and branches of thick trees, to make booths."

These booths were like the little houses that were built in the fields at harvest time, so the farmer could sleep with one eye open to catch thieves. The booths also recalled the Hebrews' wanderings in the desert after their exodus from

Egypt, when they had built rough huts to live in. During the festival all the people lived in the booths.

Sukkoth is still celebrated today, by the Jewish people in Israel and by Jews everywhere. Succahs are built in gardens, on roofs, on porches. Or, in the cities, a succah may be built at the synagogue, with everyone helping. Succahs are decorated, usually by the children, with strings of bright berries, wreaths of long-lasting flowers, grapes from the vine, and other fruits. The roof of branches should have spaces through which the stars can be seen and the rain can come, reminding the people that they must look to the heavens for protection, not to any roof.

The Feast of Lights was an ancient festival celebrated by people in a number of places, at the time when the year turns toward spring. Lighted candles were carried in procession; they represented the life-giving power of the sun. This festival was also connected with the return of the god or goddess from the underworld, and the rebirth of nature in the spring.

The Jewish festival called Hanukkah suggests this earlier Festival of Lights. It is held in December, at about the time of the winter solstice. At Hanukkah candles are lighted in the Temple and at home. But Hanukkah has always been primarily a festival celebrating a great event in Jewish history which took place more than a thousand years after the Hebrew people settled in Palestine following their escape from Egypt. This event was the victory of a brave band of Jews called Maccabees over Antiochus the Syrian, who had conquered their country.

Antiochus had taken over the Temple in Jerusalem and

forbidden the Jews to worship their God. When the Temple was retaken the people wanted to kindle the Eternal Light that had always burned inside it. There was only enough oil to last one day, yet it burned for eight. Because of this miracle, the Hanukkah festival lasts eight days.

Except for Sukkoth, the major Jewish festivals have lost most of their agricultural meaning. But behind the festivals there is still the remembrance of the promise given them by God in the far distant past. It is written in the Bible: "While the earth remaineth, seedtime and harvest, and cold and heat, and summer and winter, and day and night, shall not cease."

6

Roman Festivals

WEST OF GREECE AND PALESTINE ON THE MEDITERRANEAN Sea is Rome, the great Italian city which was the center of an empire in ancient times. Many lands were conquered by Rome. The Roman Empire lasted from the first century B.C. to the fifth century A.D. It came to include all the countries bordering on the Mediterranean Sea, and many others.

In early times the Roman calendar began the year in March. January and February were simply omitted in the old calendar, because this was a "dead season," when there was neither planting nor harvesting. The month of March was dedicated to Mars, who was an agricultural god as well as god of war. Priests of Mars, called Salii, or Leapers, took part in dancing processions over and over again during March. Singing, they marched about the city, stopping here and there to dance. The clashing of their shields and swords resounded loudly through the streets.

These processions were quite warlike, but the dances

were also intended to help the growth of the newly planted grain. It was thought that high leaps would make the grain grow high. The processions and dances were repeated in October, when grain was planted again.

The Romans had many agricultural festivals and ceremonies. There were ceremonies for Ceres, goddess of the grain. (She was the Roman form of Demeter and our word

Figure of Roman boy celebrating Floralia

cereal comes from her name.) Ceres was called upon in the spring to protect the newly planted seeds. Cakes were offered to the goddess and a fat sow was killed as a sacrifice. The Romans felt that gifts must be given to the spirits of earth, providers of fruits and grain. Otherwise, in their anger, they might make the earth a lifeless desert.

At the end of April and in early May the festival called Floralia was celebrated in honor of Flora, goddess of the flowering plants. This was originally a country feast celebrating the blossoms that came with springtime. Later, in Rome, the Floralia was celebrated by children who went to the temple of Flora wearing garlands of spring flowers on their heads and carrying flowers in their arms. The children wound their garlands around a marble column in the temple and left flowers on the altar as an offering to the goddess. Then they danced around the column, singing songs of praise.

Many years later, in England and other countries of Europe, children danced around a pole every first of May. In some places they still do. These children may never have heard of Flora, but they, too, are celebrating the blossoming world of springtime. You can read more about May Day in another chapter of this book.

In October Ceres was honored again, in a harvest festival. As in the spring, a fat sow was killed for the goddess. The first cuttings of the harvest were offered to her, in a spirit of thankfulness. There was music and dancing, sports and a feast.

The gayest festival in Rome was the Saturnalia, held in December at about the time of the winter solstice, the shortest day of the year. For the earliest people, this was an anxious time of wondering whether the days might keep on growing shorter until the sun disappeared from the sky. But to the Romans it was a time to look ahead and rejoice. Though there were cold winter days ahead, the people knew that each day after the solstice would be a little longer, and spring would surely follow.

The Saturnalia honored Saturn, god of the sowing of the grain. Saturn was said to have been a genial king of Italy a long time before. While he was on earth he taught people to till the soil. His festival lasted for seven days, and during this time schools were closed, no business was carried on, no wars were declared, no battles fought. People wore garlands of ivy. Everyone feasted, everyone was gay.

Saturnalia was a topsy-turvy time. Slaves changed places with their masters and sat at table, clad in their masters' clothes, while their masters brought them food. No one cared if the slaves complained about the service they received. This was their yearly chance to rule the household.

Besides entertaining his slaves, each householder kept open house and invited all the guests he could find. Presents were exchanged, among them wax tapers and dolls made of terra cotta, a reddish clay.

In later times, some of the customs of the Saturnalia were transferred to the Christian festival called Christmas.

Rome was sacked and burned by Vandals from the North of Europe in the fifth century A.D. This was the end of the Roman Empire and of the ancient period of history. Many of the customs of the people of Rome were forgotten. But some of the seasonal ceremonies and festivals from both Greece and Rome lived on among the country people of Europe. They, too, felt a need to express their feelings of wonder and fear and thankfulness in the presence of the natural world around them.

7

Rites of Northern People

THE VANDALS WHO DESTROYED ROME BELONGED TO A NATION of Germanic people. There were other Germanic nations in northern Europe, including, among others, Goths, Franks, and Scandinavians (or Norsemen). These people are often referred to as "barbarians," and in fact they were then rather crude and wild as compared with the people of the countries to the south on the Mediterranean Sea. Most of the Mediterranean countries had known agriculture throughout ancient times and even before. The people of northern Europe had been a wandering people; they began to settle on farms only a few hundred years before the fall of Rome.

These northern people had a great influence on the first part of the period of European history which we call the Middle Ages, a period which extended from the fall of Rome to the beginning of modern times about one thousand years later.

Germanic people worshiped nature and celebrated the

seasons, as did people everywhere. But their ways of doing so differed from those of people to the south. Winters were cold and long in the north, and the wind blew hard. Northern people believed that their windy world had been created by Odin, father of all the gods, and his two brothers. Odin rode an eight-footed swift horse and two black ravens flew about him.

Thor's hammer

Thor was the northern god of farmers. Thunder roared and lightning flashed when he threw his magic hammer into the air. Together with Odin he made the wild tempests that raged across the land.

The people of the North had great respect for nature. They were convinced that man ought not to make great changes in the earth. To do so was not only wicked but very dangerous. Yet farming *did* change the earth. When these people became farmers they surrounded every act of plowing, sowing, and harvesting with rites and spells to pacify the injured spirits of the earth. To be safe, they put all agriculture under the protection of the windy gods.

Some tribes rode horses furiously over their fields before plowing, to imitate a storm. This would please Odin, they thought. Horses' skulls were placed at the four corners of each field, because horses were sacred to Odin.

The act of plowing, of cutting and turning over the earth, filled all the northern people with terror. To escape the anger of the earth, they pretended that the plow was an animal, not a tool. They called it pig's nose, bear, or wolf. That way they could blame an animal for the tearing of the earth.

At the first plowing of the year an egg was placed on the ground before the plow. If it broke, the earth accepted it as a gift and plowing could begin.

When autumn came at last and the field was covered with waving grain, ready for the harvest, still more dangers awaited the farmer. In the rustling of the grain he heard unseen riders hunting through the fields, or witches twisting about. Gigantic animals, all invisible, might be there, great pigs, foxes, tremendous hares. A restless wind was called a buck. The brightness of the noonday sun on the fields was the "Corn Mother," going about her field, ready to burn the hearts of the people with her fiery breath.

Still, the farmer must harvest his fields. Fearfully he sharpened his sickle and ran shouting into the fields, slashing the grain. To him this was a war against the earth.

There were special rituals for the last sheaf of grain. In some places it was tied, then "taken prisoner," dressed in clothes, and placed on a wagon, where women danced around it, hooting and mocking. This was a triumph for the people; they had defeated the spirits of the grain. In other places the last sheaf was honored. It was given to a traveling stranger to take along. Who knew if he might not be Odin himself? Or the sheaf might be strewn over the field, giving back to the earth a little of its own.

Once the grain was in the storehouse, the farmers trembled as autumn winds raged, raising clouds of dust. Odin wanted his share of the grain! From the roofs of their houses people emptied sacks of flour into the wind, crying out,

> There you are, wind!
> Cook meal for your child!

The anger of the gods must be appeased. Otherwise there would be no peace on long winter nights as the farmers waited for the warmth of springtime.

part II

Pagan Rites of Europe Become Christian

Prelude

THE COMING OF CHRISTIANITY TO EUrope brought great changes in religious rites and festivals. In its early years the Christian Church had few members and they were often persecuted by the pagans among whom they lived. Then, in the fourth century A.D., the Roman Emperor Constantine, himself a Christian, declared that all men had the right to follow the religion of their choice. His successor, Theodosius, decreed that everyone must be a Christian; no one could participate in pagan rites and ceremonies. The whole Roman calendar of festivals and related events was abolished. A calendar of Christian festivals was to take its place.

This should have been the end of the dancing in the streets to honor Mars, the garlands of flowers brought by the children to the temple of Flora, the gay abandon of the Saturnalia, and all the rites that were meant to bring forth a good harvest from the earth.

But though the outward form of most of the festivals and rituals was changed, the priests of the Church could not force the people to give them up entirely. For thousands of years people had performed rites for the Earth Mother and all the gods and spirits of the natural world. Though now they might worship only one God, as did the Jews, they would not give up these rites.

The priests told them that they need not be concerned about the spirits of the earth, of seedtime and harvest. God had given to man the care of the earth. The people were not quite sure that this was true. So the priests of the Church tactfully adapted the Christian festivals to pagan rites and beliefs. Christ himself took the place of the god or goddess who died and was reborn, bringing the rebirth of nature.

The Earth Mother of earlier times blended with Mary, the mother of Christ. Some of the ancient rites and customs became part of the Christian year. Many lost their religious meaning but lived on among the people just the same.

All of these changes took place slowly, over a long period of time. Many of our festivals of today have their roots in the rites and ceremonies of the distant past. That is what the next chapters are about.

8

The Turn of the Year

FOR MORE THAN FIFTEEN HUNDRED YEARS THE BIRTH OF Christ has been celebrated by Christians on December 25. No one knows the real date of Christ's birth, but there were good reasons for choosing December 25 for the Mass of Christ, or Christmas. As we have seen, many people have celebrated the time of the winter solstice, when the sun begins to move a little higher each day as it crosses the sky, and the days begin to grow longer.

The gay Saturnalia, the Roman celebration of the winter solstice, ended on the twenty-third of December. In Persia, the twenty-fifth had long been a sacred day in honor of the birth of the Sun God, Mithras. Other rites held on this day were meant to drive away evil spirits. All had the purpose of making sure that the sun's warmth would indeed increase, bringing the springtime. This was a victory of light over darkness. Christians believed that the birth of Christ represented a victory of light over darkness in the lives of men. There could not be a more appropriate time for a festival in honor of this event.

Some Christians nevertheless refused to celebrate Christmas, condemning it as a pagan rite. Actually, in many places, the rites were still much the same as those of the ancient sun worship, in which people celebrated the rebirth of the sun as giver of life. It was hundreds of years before Christmas was widely accepted. Even then customs and beliefs from earlier times clustered around it. The rejoicing itself was timeless. Feasting and decoration of houses with greenery and lights had been part of the Roman New Year's Day. The exchanging of presents was typical of the Saturnalia as well as New Year's.

The people of northern Europe had somewhat different customs at this time of year, but these customs were later merged with Christmas. Northern people of the Middle Ages held a Yuletide festival, with great feasts, originally in mid-November. Ghosts of long-dead ancestors were said to be present at the family feast. Fir trees and other greenery decorated the houses. Gifts were exchanged and carols were sung.

December in the north was a dark month, though it held a promise of longer days to come. Fires and candles brightened Yuletide celebrations. In Sweden the festivities began with "Little Yule," on December 13, Saint Lucia's Day. A Lucia Queen was elected in each village. Dressed in white, with a crown of lighted candles on her head, the Queen set forth in the dark with a man on horseback, followed by maids of honor and "star-boys" representing demons and trolls who had been conquered by the reviving sun. The procession visited houses, farms, and stables, bringing a little of the warmth and light that was to come.

On Christmas Eve a huge "Yule candle" was lighted and

Figure of Santa Lucia

allowed to burn all night and all of Christmas day, or even until New Year's or later. Then it was put out by the head of the household. Today we light electric candles on our Christmas trees; still, these are relics of the Yule candle.

As a part of the Yuletide festivities in Europe, a Yule log was placed on the hearth, sometimes decorated with greenery and bright ribbons. It was kindled with the remains of the Yule log of the year before, which had been kept just for the purpose. Part of this year's log would be kept for the next year. The ashes might be scattered on the fields to help bring a good crop from the earth.

Yule log customs varied from place to place. In parts of France the log was cut from a fruit tree and carried three times around the kitchen before being laid on the hearth. The father of the family then poured wine over it, crying, "Joy! Joy! May God shower joy upon us, my dear children!" In chorus all the family replied, "Joy! Joy! Joy!" as they lifted the log into the fireplace. When the first flame leaped up the father said, "Burn the log, O fire!" This was not just a command to the fire. It was a prayer for the warm days of springtime.

Everywhere, Christmas or Yuletide was a festive season celebrating the lengthening days and the hope of new life to come.

Our New Year's Day comes so soon after Christmas that it seems part of the same celebration, but it is a separate holiday. The date of our New Year's came from the new calendar set up by the Roman Emperor Julius Caesar. The first day of the year in Rome was the festival of Janus, the god of all beginnings and of the rising and the setting of the sun. The month of January was named for Janus. He was a two-faced god, with one face looking back at the old year, the other looking forward to the new.

In Rome the Festival of Janus was a gay and friendly day on which gifts were exchanged and good resolutions made for the coming year. The Christians changed it to one of fasting and prayer, but this custom did not last. Today New Year's, and especially New Year's Eve, is a time for rejoicing, for singing and dancing. Bells ring out the old year and ring in the new.

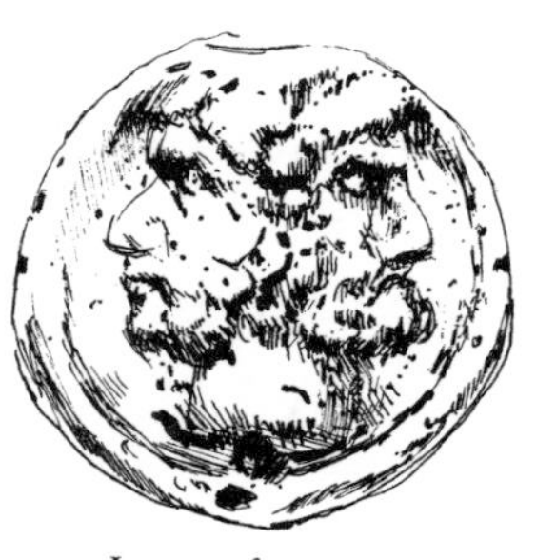

Janus, from a Roman coin

In some English villages sticks were used to help beat in the new year. Boys went out early on New Year's Day, carrying willow rods. With these they beat the apple trees as they sang this ancient song:

> Stand fast, bear well, top!
> Pray God sends us a howling crop;
> Every twig, apples big;
> Every bough, apples enow;
> Hats full, caps full,
> Full quarter sacks full.

Since they prayed for a "howling" crop, the boys were called howlers. Thus, the beginning of the year was not too soon to be thinking of harvest.

The old custom of "Wassail" belongs to New Year's Day. "Wassail" comes from the old Gaelic words *was hael,* meaning "good health." We eat together and drink together at New

Year's. Often we hear the familiar song of the poor children who once went from house to house asking for food:

> Here we come a-wassailing
> Among the leaves so green. . . .

The green leaves in the song may have come down from early Roman times, when New Year's Day was in the spring.

Everywhere New Year's is a time of fresh beginnings, looking toward spring. We make resolutions for the year ahead, with the best intentions in the world.

There is an old proverb:

> God speed the plow
> And give us bread enow.

In England work on the farms started again after a recess that began on Christmas and ended on the twelfth night thereafter. The first Monday after that was Plow Monday. Plows that were to be used in preparing the fields for the spring sowing were blessed at the church and decorated gaily. A group of young men called Plow Bullocks, wearing brightly colored ribbons from head to toe and bunches of wheat in their hats, dragged a plow from house to house, collecting contributions of money which they would later spend making merry in a tavern.

There were wild dances around the plow, a sort of acting out of the revival of the earth in spring. The Plow Bullocks jumped high, then higher and higher. The grain was supposed to grow as high that year as the dancers jumped.

In some places the plow, or just a log, was dragged over the fields in a symbolic plowing, to make sure the earth would be fertile when the time came for real plowing.

Plow Monday was also a time for a Mummers' Play with gay masked players and for the Sword Dance. This dance was originally part of a drama celebrating the rebirth of nature. There was much clashing and thrusting of swords by the dancers. Then a chain of swords was formed and finally swords were woven together in a figure called the lock, which was held high by the leader.

The climax of the dance was a beheading scene. A character in the dance, often the one called the Fool, appeared to be decapitated by the swords. As he lay still on the ground, a shout went up for a doctor, "a ten-pound doctor!" A "doctor" arrived and the Fool was revived with something from a bottle.

Mummers' Plays and Sword Dances took place at other festivals, especially at Christmas and Easter. The dances are sometimes performed even today. There are many variations in the pattern of the action, with different characters taking the part of the victim, but the central feature is always a pretend death and resurrection by magic. Just so, for countless centuries, the rebirth of nature in the spring has seemed like magic.

9

Winter Dies and Spring Comes

IN EARLIEST TIMES, AS WE HAVE SEEN, PEOPLE ENGAGED IN rites to honor the Earth Mother, so she would bring the springtime. Though she was no longer worshiped directly in later times, she was not entirely forgotten. For thousands of years people had believed that the Earth Mother, or a god of vegetation, had the power to bring green plants to the earth each year, or to withhold them. This belief remained in the later springtime rites, unrecognized perhaps, but there just the same.

In the Middle Ages in Europe there was much feasting when spring was on the way. A special loaf was baked and part was set aside for the spirits who were thought to share in the festivities. People danced with high leaps, so the grain would grow tall. There was a song about this:

> If you do not higher leap
> At harvest time you'll surely weep.

Rites were performed to frighten away the demons of winter and help bring in summer. Sometimes a battle between Summer and Winter was acted out. In some villages a man dressed in leaves, with flowers on his head, represented Summer. He fought with Winter, a man dressed in straw. Summer won and Winter was thrown down and stripped of his straw, which was torn to pieces and scattered about. Young people sang about this victory and then went from house to house carrying leaves or flowers, asking a gift of eggs and bacon.

In other places Winter wore fur, Summer was dressed all in white and carried a sickle.

Often an enormous effigy of Winter was made of straw and this was called Death. It was dragged through the streets in a spirit of mock solemnity. Then it was carried outside the village, torn apart, and burned there, or it might be buried or thrown into a river, while people cheered wildly.

After the destruction of Winter young people would cut down a young tree, trim it with green, red, and white ribbons, and hang on it a doll dressed as a woman to represent Summer. Or they would gather green branches. Singing triumphantly, they would march back to the village, carrying the tree or the branches.

Here are the words of one song they sang:

> Now carry we Death out of the village,
> The new Summer into the village,
> Welcome, dear Summer,
> Green little corn.

In England the battle between Summer and Winter developed into wild football games. A village would be divided into two teams, each with the aim of somehow kicking the ball into its own territory, or goal, by a certain time of day. Violence often ensued; torn coats, lost hats, broken shins and heads, were common.

Sometimes the struggle took the form of a mammoth tug-of-war with thousands of cheering people pulling a rope three inches thick and thirty-six yards long. In time these games became so ferocious that they have now been given up almost entirely.

Morris dances were performed in English villages, too. These dances have a long and colorful history. One dance is called Bean Setting. The dancers stamp hard on the earth to waken it. They raise up the sticks they hold in their hands, then thrust them down as if making holes in the earth to receive the seed.

The rhythmic jingling of bells in the Morris dance is also supposed to help waken the earth. The dancers raise their hands high and wave handkerchiefs. Then they leap as high as they can, hoping the grain will grow just as high. Often the dance finishes with a shout.

Like the sword dances, the Morris dances grew out of fertility rites so old that no one knows their origin. "Morris men" are now keeping these dances alive in England, and they are sometimes performed in the United States, too.

The rituals of early spring were once taken very seriously. People were convinced that if they did not do their part, the sun might not warm the earth or the green plants continue to grow from it.

Where the old rites linger on today, however, they are usually performed just as entertainment. In some places they have been revived for their historical interest or for their picturesqueness. Few people now believe that spring will not come if the rites are not performed. But there was some truth in the old ways, even so. They serve to remind us that our lives will always depend on the sun and the rain and the green plants that grow from the earth.

As the influence of the Christian religion grew, during the Middle Ages in Europe, spring rites and celebrations came to follow a general pattern prescribed by the Church. Merrymaking was allowed up until Ash Wednesday, the first day of Lent, a somber period of fasting and prayer in preparation for Easter.

The last days before Lent were usually the time for the processions and merrymaking called Carnival. The custom of a Carnival procession goes back to early times. In northern and central Europe an image of the Earth Mother was driven about the countryside in a "ship-cart," a wagon built in the shape of a ship. Sometimes, instead, a plow was carried in the cart, as a symbol of the Earth Mother. There was dancing and often the people wore strange masks.

In ancient Greece the ship-cart processions honored Dionysus, god of wine and fertility. The Romans had a similar celebration.

The Christian Church established its own ritual in February on the feast day called Candlemas. In place of the Earth Mother an image of Mary, the mother of Christ, is carried through the church in solemn procession, with lighted candles. (This ritual is also related to the early Feast of Lights which was mentioned in connection with the Jewish Hanukkah.)

Carnival itself did not die, however. Some European

cities became famous for their gay Carnivals. Many towns and villages still have such celebrations. In some, an effigy representing the Carnival is burned when the procession is over. This again means the death of Winter.

Carts are decorated with masses of flowers. People on the carts throw blossoms at the people watching in the streets. If they can catch the flowers they throw them back.

In the United States, pre-Lenten carnivals are celebrated in some southern cities; the New Orleans Mardi Gras is the most famous. Mardi Gras is French for "fat Tuesday"; it refers to the day before the beginning of Lent, when fats had to be used up because they could not be used during Lent. (Another name for this day is Shrove Tuesday.)

Mardi Gras in New Orleans means dancing at beautiful balls almost every night, and many parades, two big ones on the day itself. Floats with huge models made of papier-mâché move slowly down the street.

Myths and legends of long ago are represented on the floats. There are nymphs, serpents, mermaids, and other fantastic creatures. Black horses prance. Masked men on the floats wear colorful costumes of silk and velvet. Rex, the king of the Carnival, sits proudly on his golden throne wearing a gold-embroidered robe, his crown glittering with bright jewels.

The men on the floats throw strings of beads, ornaments, and bags of candy into the crowd. And such crowds! Almost everyone is in costume; there are gay clowns and red devils and all sorts of animals. The sound of voices blends to a happy roar, punctuated by whistles, and everywhere, it seems, there is a tinkle of tiny bells.

That evening there is the parade of Comus, Roman god of

joy, the most dearly loved of all the kings of Mardi Gras. The floats are lit with the dancing light of torches.

On the Saturday before Mardi Gras the school children of New Orleans have their own parade and their own king and queen. Floats are designed and built in the school workshops, by the children themselves.

Carnival today may seem far removed from the early rituals for the Earth Mother. Probably few of the people who take part know anything at all about the long history of this welcome to the coming springtime. The religious meaning of the day is all but smothered in color and laughter.

The Easter we celebrate today had its origin in the earliest festivals in honor of the rebirth of the natural world. Every tree and bush, every blade of grass, every flower, is part of the miracle of life which we celebrate each spring. The word Easter comes from *Eastre,* the goddess of the spring in northern Europe. The festival of Eastre became, for Christians, a celebration of the joyous day, so long ago, when Christ, who had been crucified and buried, rose from the dead.

The date of Easter set by the Church was the Sunday after the first full moon following the spring equinox, about March 21, when day and night are of equal length. It is never before March 22 or later than April 25.

Easter is closely linked with the Jewish Passover, which comes at about the same time in the spring. Saint Paul urged Christians to keep the feast with "the unleavened bread of sincerity and truth."

This was also approximately the time of the New Year's Festival in Mesopotamia and elsewhere in the Near East.

Christ himself took the place of the god in ancient mythology who died and then returned to earth, bringing new life to the world. Christ brought new life to the hearts of men.

Some of our Easter customs seem to have nothing whatever to do with religion. Yet they, too, may have their roots in the rites and mythology of the distant past.

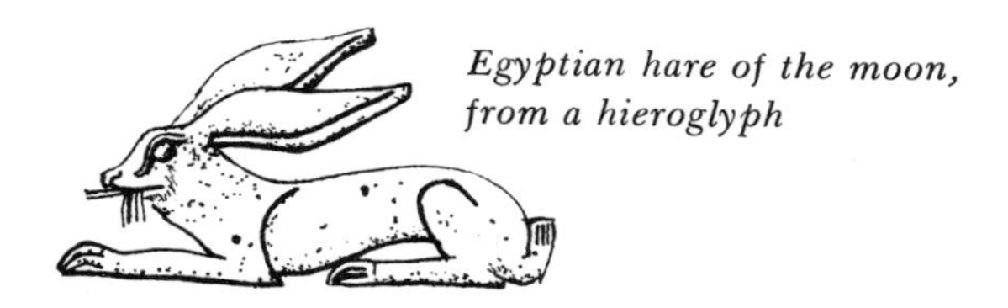

Egyptian hare of the moon, from a hieroglyph

The Easter bunny can be traced back to ancient Egypt, where the hare was a symbol of the moon. The date of Easter depends on the moon. We have a legend that says the white bunny-of-the-moon brings Easter eggs to children.

The egg is a symbol of new life, for though it does not look alive it can carry within itself the beginning of a life. A story in ancient mythology tells of a World-Egg from which came all the life on earth. Its shell was the arch of the sky. Perhaps our Easter eggs come to us from this early World-Egg.

The egg also plays an important part in the ritual of the Seder, the ceremonial meal held on the first night of the Hebrew Passover. There it is a symbol of life and hope.

An old myth says that the sun danced round and round for joy at dawn on Easter morning. Perhaps this is why people used to go to the hills at sunrise to see the sun whirling around; they declared it really did.

Water to early people was a symbol of health and a new life. According to an ancient myth, the world began in water.

Water rites have come down from early times, to be performed by people today on Easter. In many parts of Europe girls wash their faces in brooks and rivers on Easter morning. This fresh water is the water of life.

Thirty-seven days after Easter comes the Rogation ceremony, originally kept for three days. Part of this ceremony was a procession to bless the harvest, "new seed, young flocks and the husbandmen of the vineyards." The procession moved around the boundaries of the parish while the fields were blessed. Though the ceremony was introduced by a bishop about fifteen hundred years ago, its roots go much farther back, to Roman ceremonies at the same time of year, designed to protect the newly sown crops and to invoke the blessing of the goddess Ceres on the fruits of the earth.

We will probably never know how many of our songs and games have come down to us from early rites and ceremonies. Children join hands and sing:

> Oats, peas, beans and barley grow,
> Oats, peas, beans and barley grow. . . .

This was once part of a ceremony to help the crops grow. And so life continues, seedtime and harvest, year after year.

10

From Spring to Summer

MAY DAY MEANS SPRINGTIME, AND THE MAYPOLE IS ITS SYMBOL. Long streamers of many colors hang from the top of the pole. Children hold the ends of the streamers and dance around the pole, partners skipping past each other in a Grand Right and Left. As the children dance, the streamers are woven together around the pole. Then the dancers reverse their direction and the streamers unwind.

The children sing:

Round and round the maypole
    Merrily we go,
Singing hip-acherry,
    Dancing as we go.

There are many variations of this song, and many stanzas.

The dance with streamers around the maypole takes place mainly in England and in some parts of the United States. This particular way of dancing around the pole is not a very old custom. But May Day itself has as long a history as any celebration of the renewal of the earth in springtime.

In early times, in many places, trees were worshiped. It was thought that the spirit of the tree could bring new life to people in the springtime, when the tree itself put forth fresh green leaves. So trees were cut down in May and brought into the village or set up before people's houses.

The ancient Romans had their Floralia, the festival in which children wound garlands of flowers around a column in a temple. Another custom of the Floralia was the decorating of houses with flowering branches.

In England May Day became a public holiday. It had a special meaning there as the anniversary of the death of England's favorite outlaw, Robin Hood. Part of the celebration honored him and his Maid Marian.

Soon after midnight on May Day, in England and on the continent of Europe, young people went into the woods. There they played games and gathered branches of "may," or hawthorn, a prickly tree with pink and white blossoms. These they would leave at the homes of friends at dawn. Just so, even today, children may leave baskets of spring flowers hanging on doors on May Day morning.

In the woods, too, the young people cut down a tall tree and lopped off its branches, leaving a few at the top. This was their maypole. Blowing horns and flutes as they went, they took the pole back to the village.

Sometimes the maypole was over sixty feet high, more than ten times higher than a tall man. It was carried in a wagon drawn by many pairs of oxen with garlands of flowers on their horns and was placed where all could see it, usually on the village green. Some poles were painted red and white in spirals, colors that were thought to symbolize the renewal of life.

There was rejoicing as the maypole was put up, and all the young people danced around it. A May Queen was brought to the village green, often in a cart decorated with leaves and flowers and drawn by young men or maids of honor. There she was crowned.

In earlier times there was a May King, too, called Jack-in-the-Green. He was usually a chimney sweep, and he wore a wooden framework entirely covered with green leaves.

Later, only the Queen was crowned, while Jack-in-the-Green led a merry band of chimney sweeps in the May Day parade. They danced and sang and collected pennies from the crowd. Milkmaids paraded with their cows, all trimmed with ribbons. Morris dancers with bright streamers and bells did their spring dances.

Processions and ceremonies in which winter was buried and summer welcomed were sometimes a part of May Day. Any day in the month might be chosen for May celebrations.

On the first of May in England girls rise at dawn, as they have for centuries, and walk barefoot through woods and fields. There they wash their faces in the first dew of May. This, it is thought, will keep their faces beautiful all through the year. An old rhyme says:

> The fair maid who, the first of May,
> Goes to the fields at break of day,
> And washes in dew from the hawthorn tree
> Will ever after handsome be.

Today it is usually only the children and young people who celebrate May Day. In some cities in the United States the school children have their own celebrations, complete with pole and dancing in the parks. On many college campuses a May Queen is crowned.

May Day customs of course vary from place to place. In Greece all the schools are closed and everyone goes to the woods to gather wild flowers and make them into wreaths. Girls in long white robes do the graceful dances that Greek girls have done for centuries. These dances are performed in some cities in the United States, too, by groups of Greek people who have settled there.

In Italy there are sports meets and contests on May Day. In Switzerland a May Pine Tree is planted by young men before their sweethearts' windows. Danish lovers exchange bouquets of lily of the valley.

In Japan women wave branches of cherry blossoms in a dance. In Burma there are people who dance around a pole as part of their seedtime festival in the spring.

Everywhere May is a time for love and gaiety, because spring has come at last to the earth.

For centuries people in Europe have also celebrated the springtime by lighting fires. These might be new fires kindled at the family hearth, or great bonfires lit on the hillsides to drive away witches and to help the sun with its task of warming the earth.

In countries where most of the people followed the Catholic religion, all the lights were put out in the churches on Easter Eve. A new fire was then kindled, usually by rubbing flint (a kind of hard rock) on steel and letting the sparks fall into tinder, which burns readily. The great Easter candle of the church was lit from the fire that was kindled in this way, and all the lights that had been extinguished were rekindled. So, too, the sun seemed to make a new beginning in the springtime. People who were warmed by the sun felt this new beginning in themselves.

The fact that the fire was rekindled by the simple means of flint on steel tells us that the custom goes back to rituals of much earlier times.

May Day Eve in many parts of medieval Europe was called Walpurgis Night. This was the night, of all others, when witches were thought to be abroad. Men had to be on their guard. They sought to drive the witches away with loud noises, the clashing of metal instruments, playing of flutes, ringing of bells. They cracked whips and beat the ground with boards at crossroads to thrash the witches. And they lit fires.

On Walpurgis Night the Celts who had lived in Scotland and Ireland since ancient times would make a fire in the masses of shrubs called gorse, to burn out the witches. This was part of the Celtic fire festival called Beltane.

The word Beltane means "bright fire." Getting rid of witches was only one purpose of the Beltane Fire Festival. Great bonfires were built on the hills on the first day of May or soon thereafter. These fires represented the sun itself. Warmed by the many fires, the sun would surely do its good work of helping the grain to grow in the fields all through the summer. In earlier times animals were sacrificed to the sun in these fires, and before that human beings were sacrificed. Certain people were thought to be witches who should be burned in order to keep evil away. Sacrificing them meant, too, a gift to the sun, so the seasons would not fail to follow one after the other.

People danced around the Beltane fires, leaping as high as they could so the grain would grow high. In their dancing they moved in the same direction the sun followed as it crossed the sky. They ran around the fields carrying burning brands from the fire; they rolled blazing wheels across the fields. This, it was thought, would help the earth to produce a good crop. Witches would be driven away, too. With the same purpose, embers were scattered on the fields.

Cattle were driven through the fires to protect them from disease. Young people leaped through a fire, or between two fires, with great shouts, for good luck. Doing this would also help drive out the witches. "Fire, fire! Burn the witches!" the jumpers shouted.

Huge round cakes of oatmeal were rolled downhill in some districts. These were Beltane cakes, and they, too, represented the sun. When the festival was over the cakes were divided up among the people.

There were always fires in people's houses, for warmth on cold days and for cooking every day. These were put out just before Beltane. Branches were then lit in the Beltane fires on the hillsides and carried into the houses to kindle new fires on the hearths. This, too, was an ancient ceremony, marking a new beginning.

Beltane festivals ceased to be observed in Scotland and Ireland about two hundred years ago. Here and there May fires are built on the hillsides, but the meaning is not the same. The sun grows warmer every springtime, the grain grows, and witches stay away, without the rituals of men.

New-fire ceremonies are still held in country places in some parts of the world. The old fire on the family hearth is put out and a new one is kindled, as a symbol of a new beginning.

Even more important as a time for fire rites, over a wider area, was Midsummer Eve, on June 23. June 24 was called the summer solstice (we now, more accurately, date it on June 21 in the Northern Hemisphere). This is the time of year when the sun travels highest in the sky as it seems to move from east to west—the time when the days are longest. The night before the solstice is called Midsummer Eve.

The early Celts were at first not aware of the importance of the solstice. As we have seen, their fire ceremonies to aid the sun came in May. When they decided to celebrate the solstice, too, they simply extended their fire rituals to Midsummer Eve, with the same fires and dancing and burning wheels with which they celebrated Beltane in May.

All over Europe, and among the Moslem people of North Africa, fires were lit on Midsummer Eve. No one knows how old this custom is, but it dates back to very early times. Early man was convinced that without his help the sun might really fail to warm the earth all through the year. And everywhere in Europe people believed that Midsummer fires scared away witches.

In Switzerland burning disks, lit at the fires, were hurled into the air. In some places a tall fir tree was cut down, set up on a hill, and decorated by girls with wreaths of green leaves, blossoms, and red ribbons. Brushwood was piled around it, and when night came the brush was set on fire and the tree burned. In Sweden a Midsummer Tree was set up and decorated. The villagers danced around it, lit fires and jumped over them. For the Swedes the Midsummer Tree took the place of the maypole.

In London at Midsummer bonfires were kindled in the streets at the time of the first Queen Elizabeth in the sixteenth century. In the Vale of Glamorgan in Wales a cart wheel wound with straw was lit and sent rolling down the hill. If it kept burning all the way down, an abundant harvest was expected. In many places in the British Isles people marched around the fields carrying burning torches.

On Midsummer Day it was also the custom for women and girls to bathe in a river. Long ago this bathing was a part of magic for bringing the life-giving rain. In a river the water is always moving, always renewed. So, too, life renews itself.

The Catholic Church chose Midsummer for celebrating the birth of Saint John the Baptist and called it Saint John's Day. Saint John the Baptist was the forerunner of Jesus Christ; he baptized Jesus in the river Jordan. Jesus had once called John "a burning and a shining light." The Church told the people that Midsummer fires should represent Saint John instead of the sun. But the rites and their meaning for the people changed very little until recent times.

In many parts of Europe, in country places, fires are still lit on hills and mountains at Midsummer Eve. Some of those who watch may remember the ancient meaning of these fires.

II

Autumn Festivals

THE CELTS HELD A FESTIVAL OF BEGINNINGS ON THE FIRST OF November. This was their New Year, and the festival was called Samhain, which means "summer ends." At this time of year cattle were brought in from the pastures to spend the winter in their stalls inside the barns. The harvest had been reaped and stored. Cold days were ahead.

In winter there was a shortage of fodder for the cattle. Some animals were killed at Samhain and there was a great feast. The Beltane rites of the springtime were repeated, to usher in the winter and to please the spirits of the grain. Their aid was sought to ensure the fertility of the earth when at last spring came again. As at Beltane, fires on the hearths were put out and relighted from bonfires on the hills. In earlier times animals were sacrificed in the fires. Later, many of the rites of Samhain were transferred to the Yule Feast at Christmas. The burning yule log became part of an indoor fire festival.

There was a Festival of the Dead each year on Samhain Eve. Shivering ghosts fled the bare fields and leafless woods, seeking shelter in the cottages with their familiar firesides. They were welcomed there, just for that night.

It was said that in Ireland all the fairy hills were thrown wide open on Samhain Eve and the fairies swarmed forth. Witches and demons swept through the air; elves and goblins were everywhere about, ready to do evil to the fertile earth and the animals that lived upon it. The festival sought to please the ghosts and scare away the witches, both at once.

The Catholic Church chose the first of November as All Saints' Day, in memory of the saints of the Church. November second became All Souls' Day, when all the dead are remembered. The night before All Saints' Day was called Allhallow Eve or Halloween. Halloween, however, never became a Christian holiday. Instead, it is a time of fun and frolic, especially loved by children. Most Halloween customs date back to earlier times. Ducking for apples recalls the ancient Roman festival honoring Pomona, goddess of orchards. The bright candle lit behind a pumpkin face is reminiscent of the great bonfires lit on hillsides at Samhain. The scary witch and ghost costumes so loved by children suggest

the masquerade costumes worn by the Celts in Samhain processions to scare away evil spirits.

This was a night, too, for foretelling the future. For example, if a girl looked into a mirror while eating an apple and saw a boy peeping over her shoulder, she would surely marry him.

Some of the customs connected with the Celtic Festival of the Dead survived, too. In parts of Europe, on Halloween, lamps are still lit on graves, candles are burned in houses, bells are tolled till midnight, and "soul-cakes" are offered to the spirits of the dead.

There have been harvest rituals ever since man first planted his grain in the earth and watched it grow and ripen. As we have seen, the Celtic Samhain was partly a harvest festival, though the Church, on taking it over, emphasized only one aspect of it, the Festival of the Dead.

In some parts of Europe country people still believe in a Corn Mother, direct descendant of Demeter, the Greek goddess of the growing grain. At harvest the spirit of the Corn Mother was said to be present in the last sheaf of grain left standing in the field. Cutting this last sheaf was no easy thing, for the Corn Mother herself might be caught or killed. Sometimes the last sheaf was beaten with sticks to drive out the Corn Mother. "There she is! Hit her!" the reapers cried. When all the seeds had been threshed out of this sheaf of grain it was believed that the Corn Mother had been driven away. It was better so; she was to be feared as well as respected.

In some places the last sheaf of grain was braided and made into a doll with the shape of a woman. The doll was dressed and decked with flowers and bright ribbons. Then it was fastened to a pole and brought home with the last wagonload of grain. Whoever held the pole kept waving it so the doll wagged and wiggled as if it were alive. At the farm it was placed on the floor where the grain was threshed and kept there until the threshing was done. Thus the spirit of the Corn Mother stayed with the reapers in the doll made of grain. She would surely bring a good harvest next year.

Sometimes the ritual of the Corn Mother seemed to be taken as a joke. In eastern Europe the reaper who cut the last sheaf of grain was himself called the Corn Mother. He was covered with a dress made of sheaves of grain and trundled through the village in a wheelbarrow. Crowds of laughing people followed.

In parts of Scotland a reaper was blindfolded and whirled around until he was dizzy. Then he staggered about, trying to cut the last sheaf of grain. The others jeered and hooted at his wild attempts to swing the scythe. This game continued until a blindfolded reaper succeeded in cutting the sheaf. How like the game of pinning a tail on a donkey!

In some places the last sheaf was dressed and called the Old Woman or even the Old Man; or it might be called the Harvest Child. Sometimes the doll made from the last sheaf was thrown into the river to make sure there would be plenty of rain and dew for the next year's crop. Or, with the same ritual purpose, it was drenched with water after it was brought home.

A passing stranger might be wrapped up and tied in the last sheaf of grain. He would have to pay a forfeit before he was freed, but meanwhile, whether he would or no, he represented the Spirit of the Corn.

To people in still other areas, cutting or threshing the last sheaf seemed like killing the Corn Mother, but this became more of a game than a serious threat. In one part of Germany the men who did the threshing kept time as they beat the grain with their flails to force out the seed. As they did so they called out, "We are killing the Old Woman! We are killing the Old Woman!"

Country people in England have always loved the time of their harvest. The poet Gerard Manley Hopkins wrote about it this way:

> Summer ends now; now, barbarous in beauty,
> the stooks arise
> Around; up above, what wind-walks! what lovely
> behaviour
> Of silk-sack clouds!

The English harvest festival was called Harvest Home. The reaper who cut the last grain was lord of the harvest. As the last load, pulled by big work horses, made its way home, the reapers and their friends and sweethearts rode on top or walked alongside carrying garlands of autumn flowers and making merry. Harvest Home supper, with roast beef and ale, followed after the grain had been safely stored.

Then there was singing, sometimes with these words:

> The boughs do shake and the bells do ring,
> So merrily comes our harvest in,
> Our harvest in, our harvest in,
> So merrily comes our harvest in.

We have plowed, and we have sowed,
We have reaped, and we have mowed,
We have brought home every load,
Hip, hip, hip,

Harvest Home!

In some parts of England a harvest queen was chosen. She was decorated with the fruits of the earth and paraded through the streets in a carriage drawn by white horses, a Corn Mother honored as a queen.

The village church was often decorated with autumn flowers—marigolds, red dahlias, sunflowers—and all the autumn vegetables—potatoes, beets, onions, and pumpkins. Sheaves of wheat and barley were twisted into bouquets or made into such shapes as sickles and scythes. A loaf of bread made from the new wheat was placed on the altar, just as loaves were brought to the Temple at the Hebrew festival of Shavuoth. People came to the church to give thanks to God for the fruits of the earth.

The Pilgrims in Plymouth celebrated their first harvest in North America with a feast of thanksgiving in 1621. They had sailed across the Atlantic Ocean on the *Mayflower*, arriving in the bitter cold of December. Only half of those who came survived that first terrible winter. For those who did survive, the first harvest was indeed a time for rejoicing. The Indians had given seeds of maize (Indian corn) to the Pilgrims and it had grown well. Without those seeds there might have been no harvest to celebrate. So the Indian chief Massasoit was invited to dinner, with more than eighty of his braves.

The thanksgiving feast of the Pilgrims was not the first

harvest celebration on the continent of North America, however. Indians had celebrated their own harvests, in their own way, for hundreds of years. English settlers in Newfoundland held their first New World harvest festival forty-three years before the Pilgrims, and the Popham Colony in what is now Maine celebrated fourteen years before the Pilgrims.

The Thanksgiving of the Pilgrims nevertheless became the pattern everywhere in the United States. The Pilgrims feasted on the turkeys that ran wild in the woods. So Thanksgiving dinner today must include a turkey, though no longer a wild one. There are apples and apple cider, pumpkin pie, nuts to crack, and an abundance of all the fruits of autumn.

The date of Thanksgiving was not the same in each of the New England colonies, but today, in all fifty states, it is always celebrated on the fourth Thursday in November.

Thanksgiving in Canada is on the second Monday in October, at the close of the harvest season. On Sunday, the day before, churches are decorated with the fruits of the harvest and the people gather to give thanks, much as they do in England at Harvest Home. On Monday there is a feast and usually its main feature is—again—turkey.

Thanksgiving today lacks the ritual of earlier times that was meant to bring an abundant harvest the following year or to make certain that enough rain would fall. But it is in the same tradition, nevertheless. The wonder and the magic is in the hearts of the people as they gather around to partake of the abundance produced by the good earth.

part III

Rites and Ceremonies of Other Continents

Prelude

SO FAR THIS BOOK HAS DEALT WITH RITES and ceremonies of only a small part of the world. These are important to many people in Europe and the United States today as part of their heritage from the past. Among us in the United States, however, live people with a quite different heritage—American Indians who inhabited North America long before the white men came, Mexicans from across our southern border, black people whose ancestors came from Africa, Chinese and Japanese from the other side of the world. And many others.

Today, too, we are in touch with other parts of the world to a greater extent than ever before. The time is past when any place on earth is really far away. Radio sends news around the world almost as fast as it happens. People who live on other continents, even on deserts and in remote jungles, appear on our television screens. Jet planes carry passengers across the wide oceans in hours. People everywhere are our neighbors.

All of us have the same basic human needs—food and clothing for our bodies, shelter from the rain and the cold, a chance to feel we are needed in the world. But there are significant differences, too, and among these are the differences in the rites and ceremonies that are a part of the life of the people.

Throughout many centuries people in most parts of the world have developed their own rites and ceremonies for hunting, seedtime and harvest, for rain making, and for celebration of the changing seasons. The pattern of rites for each group of people grew out of their own particular way of looking at the world they saw around them and the world they felt within themselves. We know these people better when we know something about their rites and ceremonies.

All of these ceremonies have their roots in the distant past. Some are still performed today; because the world is changing rapidly, some are not. All of them can help us to understand people who see the world from a point of view different from our own.

12

Africans Celebrate Sowing and Harvest

AFRICA IS A BIG CONTINENT. WE ARE CONCERNED IN THIS chapter only with the part of Africa that lies south of the Sahara Desert, but that is more than half of it. Except in the far southern part of this area, the climate is tropical, warm all year round. There is no real summer or winter. Instead, there are rainy seasons and dry seasons. The time of planting and harvest depends on these seasons.

The plants that grow from the earth flourish in the rainy seasons. In the dry seasons few plants can grow. The land nearest the equator is the wettest, usually with two rainy seasons and two dry seasons each year. This is the general pattern of the climate, and it is helpful to keep it in mind. But there are places in Africa that do not fit into this pattern. The land is too varied for that.

Africa south of the Sahara has a long history. Ruins of cities of early African civilizations have been excavated, some of them dating back to several hundred years before

Christ. Great empires flourished in Africa during the Middle Ages. Trading ships crossed the Mediterranean Sea, carrying goods between Europe and the African empires.

In recent years life in Africa has been changing rapidly, and in many places the beliefs you will read about in this chapter are no longer held. Customs that are ages old are being given up, among them religious customs. Tribal ceremonies are often no longer performed.

Some Africans are Christians; they celebrate the festivals of the Church and sometimes they take part in tribal ceremonies as well. Many are Moslems and they keep the Moslem holidays. But everywhere in Africa the people know that life is brought to them by the fruits of the earth, the animals that walk on the earth, and the welcome rain. Tribal beliefs and ceremonies are still important, whether they are considered a part of the present of Africa or only a part of its past.

There are many tribes in Africa south of the Sahara. They do not all believe the same things or have the same customs. But most believe in a supreme god who is given different names by different tribes. They believe that this god created all things. He is rather far away; he seldom influences the lives of men except in times of great need.

A large number of lesser gods or spirits, varying from tribe to tribe, are thought to control the everyday life of the people. These spirits are invisible powers that control such natural forces as drought and flood, wind and sun, thunder and lightning, poor soil on worn-out fields. They influence, too, the everyday activities of life, such as fishing, raising cattle, and growing crops in the earth. These spirits take an interest in a man's behavior, rewarding him when he does right, punishing when he does wrong. They have feelings much like his own; like him they appreciate praise and kindness. Elaborate rules and ceremonies govern man's relationship to these spirits.

Even more important to the African are the spirits of the ancestors. When a person dies his soul joins the souls of other ancestors in the spirit world. The soul continues to be interested in family affairs and wishes to be consulted about them. Food is set out for the soul; words of praise are spoken. The soul, if satisfied, will bring good fortune to the family. If neglected, it can bring sickness and disaster.

Since the sun is warm in the sky all year round in tropical Africa, there are no rites and ceremonies to give strength to the sun or to ensure its return after a long winter. But African peoples have always had important ceremonies at the times of sowing and harvest. When the seeds are planted the blessing of the spirits is sought. Food may be offered to the spirits; often an animal or a fowl is sacrificed.

At the beginning of the harvest first fruits are often offered to the spirits of the ancestors. In Southwest Africa, for example, some of the new grain is made into a porridge. The head of the family takes some of the porridge, dips it in melted fat, and throws it to the east, saying, "Take it, spirits of the East!" Then he throws some of the porridge to the west, saying, "Take it, spirits of the West!" This is a thank offering to the spirits of the ancestors who have kept the people in good health while they cultivated the fields, and who have sent rain.

The ancestors are important not only to the people who grow crops in the earth. The tribes that live by herding cattle sacrifice some of their animals to the ancestors on important occasions. And the tribes that live by hunting offer to the ancestors their songs of praise and thanks.

Dancing is an important part of African ceremonies. There is a dance for every season of the year, for the sowing and reaping of each crop that grows in the earth. With the dance there is often the sound of drums beating in steady rhythm, like the beat of a human heart. The African does not just hear the rhythm of the drums; he feels it in his own body as he dances. He is lifted beyond himself, and he seems to feel the rhythm of the spirits of rocks and trees and the moving water of rivers. He feels, too, the rhythm of the spirits of the grain and other plants that grow from the earth. The dance is a message to these spirits and to the ancestors, asking them to look with favor on the people and to help them produce an abundant harvest.

The ceremonies vary greatly from place to place. An Ashanti farmer in West Africa will not plow the earth until he has asked permission of the earth spirit and the spirits of his ancestors. First he kills a fowl as a sacrifice and pours its blood on the ground. Then he cuts up the fowl, mixes it with cooked plantain or yam, and scatters it afield, to the north, south, east, and west. This is an offering to Asase Yaa, the earth spirit or earth mother, and to the spirit of the farmer's grandfather who once cultivated this land. The real owners of the land are the spirits of the ancestors who worked on it and who watch over it still.

As he makes his offering the farmer says a prayer to the earth spirit and to the spirit of his grandfather, asking for help in raising a good crop in the earth. He wants, too, to be protected from disasters such as accidents and snake bites.

The supreme god of the Ashanti is Nyame, the Sky God. But the earth spirit Asase Yaa is next in importance. Every three weeks there is a ceremony in honor of the ancestors and Asase Yaa. This message is beaten out in the rhythm of "talking drums":

> Earth, when I am about to die
> I lean upon you.
> Earth, while I am alive
> I depend upon you.

Spirits of the earth receive great honor also in other West African tribes. To some the earth mother is the most important god of all.

At the end of October comes the first-fruits festival of the Ashanti. It is a festival of yams. There are two days of ceremonies during which the ritual follows a pattern that has been the same for hundreds of years. Priests dance, accompanied by rattles, drums, and singing. Drums "talk" in the night, and the people understand their message. At the end of the ceremonies a sheep is killed as a sacrifice to the gods. Yams from the new harvest are offered to the gods and are given to the chief. Only when all this, and more, has been done can the people themselves eat of the yams. The only exception is the children, who may eat them at any time.

Among the Yoruba, another West African tribe, the yam festival is part of an annual ritual of the ancestors, who are represented by people dressed in long robes, with masks covering their faces. These masqueraders dance in the streets and visit people's houses, especially those in which someone has died during the past year, for the dancers are

Yoruba mask

the spirits of the dead. New yams are offered to the ancestral spirits before the people can eat them.

The Gã tribe of West Africa has an annual feast called hunger-hooting, when the new crop of corn is ready. Whatever is left of the previous crop is cooked and sprinkled with sacred water at the shrines of the ancestors and the gods.

The spirits are invited to eat and drink, and are asked to continue to protect the people against disease and misfortune. Then the living eat. If the harvest of the previous year was a good one, this is a great feast. No food is left over. Then, before the new corn is eaten, some must again be offered to ancestors and gods. Everyone rejoices. This is the beginning of the farmer's year and people greet one another:

> Take life, take life.
> May the year's end meet us,
> May we live to be old,
> May no black cat cross between us,
> At the end of this year may we sit again.

Most of the Kikuyu people in Kenya, East Africa, are farmers who depend entirely on the land. The earth is their mother, they say, because it nourishes them as long as they live and when they die it cares for their spirits forever.

The god of the Kikuyu, Ngai, is creator and giver of all things, including the fertile earth. His power is seen in the sun, the moon, the stars, the rain and the rainbow, the thunder and the lightning. He is a great god and does not concern himself with daily affairs. Only in serious matters do the people ask his help, and then it is asked by the family group or the whole community, not by individuals. His blessing is asked on the seeds that are planted in the earth, and thanks are offered to him for the harvest.

In Kikuyu country there are two rainy seasons and two dry seasons each year. The season of big rain lasts from March to July, the big harvest from July to early October. There is a short rainy season from October to January, and then comes the season of harvesting millet, a quick-growing grain.

The activities of all the Kikuyu people are determined by this pattern of the seasons, and the ceremonies at seed-time and harvest are at the heart of Kikuyu religious life.

The planting ceremony comes when the welcome rain has fallen, after each dry season. No one is allowed to plant his fields until this ceremony has been completed. The seeds to be planted in the ceremony are first put into calabashes (containers made from gourds) together with the contents of the stomach of a lamb that has been sacrificed.

In the early morning these calabashes are taken to a special field by four people who have been chosen to perform this ceremony: a woman who is a "mother" of the community, a respected old man, and two children.

Facing Mount Kenya, the sacred mountain of the god Ngai, the old man holds up one of the calabashes and prays to Ngai ("Mwene-Nyaga" is a way of addressing Ngai): "Mwene-Nyaga, you who have brought us rain of the season, we are now about to put the seeds in the ground; bless them and let them bear as many seeds as those of *gekonyi*." (*Gekonyi* is a creeping vine that has many seeds.)

The old man then hands some of the seeds to the woman and she gives a few to each child. The children plant the seeds, after first scratching the earth with a special digging stick that has been cut from a sacred tree.

Then the prayer is said again and more seeds are planted in the same way. The ritual is repeated until all the different kinds of seeds have been planted.

The woman, the old man, and the children return to the village. Here the horn of the planting ceremony is sounded. It is a welcome sound. Everyone who hears it knows that the planting ceremony is finished and now the people can plant their own fields.

The seeds sprout, the plants grow, and the people pull the weeds that come up around them. Then, after two or three months, the plants begin to bear their fruits—beans, corn, potatoes, and other vegetables. If there is to be a good harvest, the fields must be protected from insects. This is the time of the ceremony of purifying the crops.

A lamb is killed as a sacrifice to Ngai and roasted over the embers of a ceremonial fire which burns wood from sacred trees. Torches are brought from this fire to kindle fires beside all the fields. The crops are purified with sacred fire and smoke.

Inside every hut the family fires burn. All these fires are now put out and new fires are lit from the sacred torches. These new fires are carefully guarded; they must last until they are replaced by the sacred fire of the next season.

Thus new fire is kindled with ceremony in Kikuyu villages, as it is in many other parts of the world.

When the crops are almost ready to harvest, it is time to offer thanks to Ngai for his gift of rain, without which there would be no harvest. Again a lamb is sacrificed, and the old men say a prayer to Ngai, speaking together this chorus: "Peace, praise ye, Ngai, peace be with us."

As a part of this ceremony small storage huts are built temporarily along the main roads. These are for Ngai. When the farmer has harvested the first crop of his fields, he must put a few grains into one of these storage huts as he passes by.

The old men of the ceremonial council then cook the offerings and feast upon them. In this way Ngai will know that the gifts of the farmers are pure, good enough for anyone to eat.

Dancing plays no part in the solemn ceremonies dedicated to Ngai. No musical instruments are used, except occasionally a ceremonial horn. But the people do dance, sometimes night after night around blazing fires, in a rhythm that seems like the rhythm of life itself.

Rain making is an important religious activity in many parts of Africa. The priest who performs this ritual does not actually claim to "make" rain. Usually he invokes the blessing of the ancestors and prays to them for rain. The power to bring it is theirs, not his.

The Kikuyu pray to Ngai for rain, sacrifice a lamb, and hold a ritual procession, seven times around a sacred tree. Elsewhere in East Africa the rain maker sprinkles water that he has blessed from a new calabash. As the drops fall, so the rain may also fall. The rain song is sung:

> An arrow for the people of the Arrow,
> Swift to the figs, O Pigeons of the Rain,
> Hoes for the Hoers. (Gather, O Clansmen.)
> The flail of the thunder on the threshing-floor
> of God.

Then the people dance the rain dance, joyfully, until sunset. Their soft pattering feet imitate the sound of the first slow raindrops and then, more swiftly, with the swishing of women's skirts, the rapid falling of a steady rain.

Whether or not the rain falls when the rain dance is finished, the people can feel at peace. They have done what they can; together they have danced to please the gods. So, too, when the people perform their ceremonies at seedtime and harvest, they follow the ancient ritual for the gods and the ancestors. Then, whatever comes, they know that they face the future together.

13

Yams, Rice, and Ceremonies of the Far East

THE KAI PEOPLE OF NEW GUINEA, IN THE EAST INDIES, PLAY games to help their crops grow. Holding tight to a long reed that is fastened to a branch of a tree, they swing high in the air. This they believe will make their newly planted yams grow high. Everyone swings; old and young, men and women, boys and girls. As they swing to and fro they sing songs in which they call out the name of the kind of yam they have planted and shout joyfully in celebration of the coming harvest.

Another game to help the yams grow is playing with string figures (like cat's cradles). A Kai holds a big loop of string, or vine, taut between his hands. With the fingers of one hand he picks up loops of string from the other hand in different ways, over and over again, spreading his hands each time. In this way he can make intricate designs, all of which have a definite meaning. There are "the spider's web," "rain and sunshine," "the star," "the lizard and the dog," and many others. Playing with these string designs, the Kai believe, will make the leaves of the yam spread and the stalks wind around their stakes, just as the players spread their hands and twine the loops of string around their fingers.

Legends are told by the storytellers when the newly planted crops are sprouting, and at no other time. Telling about the powerful spirits who first created the fruits of the earth is thought to make the crops grow well. "Shoots and fruits in abundance!" says the storyteller at the end of his story.

Other tribes in New Guinea also tell tales when their crops have been planted. Some believe that a good harvest depends on the spirits of the dead, so they ask the blessing of the dead before planting. Later, they whirl bull-roarers wildly in the fields and call out the names of the dead. A bull-roarer is a specially shaped slat of wood with a thong attached to one end. It makes a loud roaring sound when it is whirled. Other tribes, too, use a bull-roarer for helping the crops to grow. It has been called "the mother of yams."

The East Indies are islands with a tropical climate; they are all located on the equator or just north or south of it. Here, as we saw in tropical Africa, there is no real summer or winter. The time of planting and reaping depends on rainy seasons and dry seasons. In much of this area, and on the mainland of Southeast Asia, the principal food of the people is rice, which needs a warm climate for growing.

Some of the people in the East Indies believe that since rice means life to them it must itself have a soul. The Indonesian farmer handles the rice with great gentleness and courtesy, believing that it will not grow well if he scares away the "bird of life," the soul of the rice. At harvest time

Rice stalk

he is especially careful of the seed that is intended for the next year's harvest. Seed that has lost its soul will not produce any crop at all. The farmer reaps the seed-rice with a special knife that has its cruel blade hidden beneath his fingers. In this way he hopes not to frighten away the soul.

Among the Kayans on the island of Borneo, west of New Guinea, masked men do a dance before the rice is sown. The men represent spirits, and their masks, with goggle eyes, huge ears, and big teeth, suggest that they are not men. Their bodies are so thickly wrapped in shredded banana leaves that they look like moving masses of green foliage.

Under the burning rays of the midday sun the men dance to the beat of gongs, leaping to make the rice grow high. Then they march away, making motions with their arms as if catching the souls of the rice, which may have wandered far away.

In the evening eight girls, also disguised, dance with slow steps and gracefully waving arms. In the same way, if the crop grows well, the stalks of rice will sway in the wind.

On the Malay Peninsula, at the southeastern tip of Asia, a particular sheaf of rice is chosen before the harvest to represent the mother of the rice-soul. From this sheaf a priestess cuts a little bundle of seven heads, ties them with colored thread, wraps them in a white cloth, and puts them in an oval-shaped basket. This bundle is the infant soul of the rice and the basket is its cradle. Another woman carries the basket to the farmer's house, shielding it from the hot sun with an umbrella. The rice-child is welcomed by the women of the family and is laid, still in its cradle, on a new sleeping-mat with pillows at the head.

The sheaf that remains standing in the field is treated gently, as if it were a new mother. It is reaped by the farmer's wife. After a few days the infant soul of the rice and the rice-mother are threshed to remove the seeds, and some grains from the rice-soul are mixed with the seed that is to be sown the following year.

At the rice harvest in Java, one of the islands of Indonesia, bundles of rice, adorned with flowers, become the rice-bride and rice-bridegroom. Their wedding feast is celebrated before the rice is cut.

The farmer in Thailand, in southeast Asia, traditionally has great respect for the soul of the rice. He marks the stages of its growth by ceremonies. When he prepares the seedbed

Indonesian rice doll

for his rice he makes an offering to the rice goddess. Bits of food, flowers, and tobacco are put in a cone of banana leaf in a corner of the seedbed.

The rice grows in the seedbed until it is a few inches high. Then the farmer transplants it in little bunches in his flooded field. When he does this he makes an offering to the Earth Mother.

Little bamboo flags are often seen in the rice fields. These are to keep away evil spirits while the rice grows, and to remind the farmer's neighbors that his rice is "pregnant" and must be left alone.

As in other parts of the world, many farmers in Thailand no longer follow the old customs. But the people dearly love festivals and there are many. There is one to celebrate the coming of the rainy season and one to mark its end. There is a festival for the coming of the New Year and one for the end of the old. One for the waxing of the moon and another for its waning.

Before the rice is planted in the spring there is an official ceremony to bless the seed. With a rolling of drums and the haunting wail of a blown conch shell, a procession of important people offers prayers to Buddha at a small wooden temple that is set up in a field. Then the Thai Minister of Agriculture, wearing a jeweled crown that tapers to a fine point, plows three circular furrows in the center of the field with an ancient wooden plow. This done, he scatters seed freely over the soil from gold and silver baskets. Three more furrows are plowed and the ground is sprinkled with holy water.

Crowds of eager people watch this ceremony. When it is finished they surge forward in a mad scramble, all reaching for a handful of the seed that has been scattered. Farmers will mix this with their own seed to ensure a good harvest.

When the rice harvest is finished in Thailand in late December, there is little work to be done in the fields. The people have time to celebrate, and feasts and festivals take place everywhere. The countryside is bright with colored banners on poles. Orchestras make gay music in the evenings. In one harvest celebration four men sit on the plank of an enormous swing hung by ropes from a wooden crosspiece. Swinging high, they try to seize in their teeth a small bag of money tied loosely to a tall bamboo pole. Crowds of people watch; they groan when the bag is missed and cheer loudly when at last it is seized. If the men fail over and over again it is believed that there will be poor rains and a bad crop.

April, during the hottest part of the year, is the time for the Buddhist festival called Songgram, lasting three days. Young people throw water on each other just for fun. Scented water is sprinkled on the statues of Buddha in temples. Rains are due soon, and this throwing of water should hurry their coming. Meanwhile the young people have cooled off considerably, inside and out.

Chinese Rituals

THE RITUALS OF THE CHINESE are among the most ancient in the world. They had their beginnings in early times when people worshiped the spirits they believed inhabited the world around them. The Chinese farmer felt very deeply his dependence on the earth. The soul of the people and the good earth were one; each needed the other. A Chinese proverb says: "Who plants a garden plants happiness."

Much has changed in China in recent years. The present government has forbidden the people to perform their rituals in the old way. All festivals must now glorify the country's leaders and inspire people to work harder for the state. That is why in this chapter Chinese beliefs and festivals are described as belonging to the past, though some may exist today in changed form. Chinese people in other parts of the world, however, remember the old ways and keep them alive as best they can.

The Chinese have a lunar calendar, each month representing about the time required for the moon to change from new to full and new again. Thus, the first month is called the First Moon, and so on. In addition to numbers, the months have names. The Moon of Hungry Ghosts (Seventh) is followed by the Harvest Moon (Eighth).

There were always many ceremonies and festival days in China. On these days the people worshiped their ancestors and heroes, the sun, the moon, and the stars. They believed that the souls of people who died went up to heaven to live with the gods on the stars, the moon, and the sun. The gods and the ancestors controlled man's world, rewarding honest people who lived in peace, took good care of their families, and respected their elders. They punished those who failed to do these things.

Festivals celebrated the seasons, too. Unlike those of many other countries and religions, early Chinese festivals did not become celebrations of great historical events. They never lost their meaning as expressions of wonder at the natural world and prayers to the spirits of that world.

Early in the Holiday (First) Moon or late in the Bitter (Twelfth) Moon, there was a holiday called Li Chum, which means "Spring is here!" (By our calendar this date is usually early in February.) The nights were still long at the time of Li Chum and it was very cold. But spring was on the way and the people celebrated the promise of its coming.

There were plowing ceremonies on the farms. Dressed in colorful embroidered robes, an official who represented the government arrived early in the morning at a field that had been chosen for the Li Chum ceremony. First, at a small shrine, he made an offering of sweets and fruit to the god of spring and the god of farming. Incense was burned. The official plowed the first furrow in the field, using the plow and oxen or water buffaloes that the farmers had brought. The farmers could then look forward to a good season.

In towns and cities on the day of Li Chum all the people (except soldiers, who were considered bad luck in the spring) marched in a big procession with flags and banners and flowers. Everyone carried a small clay image of the water buffalo. Another huge image of a buffalo was borne through the streets. Its frame was made of bamboo, a symbol of long life. Paper of different colors covered its sides.

The procession made its way to a temple. There all the clay images of the water buffalo were destroyed. The bamboo buffalo was burned; its spirit would go to heaven and plead for a prosperous season for the people.

Later, in their homes, people lit candles and burned

Chinese kitchen shrine

incense. Fruit and seeds were set out as an offering to the gods. Some people then went to performances of plays that had been given on this holiday for hundreds of years. Some went to plum-blossom parties. Others went to weddings, and there were many, since this was a lucky time to be married.

Li Chum was a happy holiday.

Late in February there was a holiday called Yu Shui, meaning "spring showers." Three weeks later came Ching Che, "the insects are stirring." Everyone ate sweets and made a game of killing the insects that ate the plants.

On the third day of the Sleepy Moon (the Third) came Ch'ing Ming, "the pure and bright festival." Its date was just 106 days after the winter solstice, when the daily path of the sun starts to move higher in the sky and the days grow longer. This festival dated back to the early days of sun worship.

Spring had really come to China. Leaves had begun to uncurl on the branches of trees, the earth was bright with early spring flowers, and the birds had flown back from the South.

Three days before Ch'ing Ming, kitchen fires in some parts of China were put out. No new fires were lit; only cold food was eaten during these three days.

When the day of the Ch'ing Ming festival itself arrived, people honored the dead. They went to the burial grounds, swept fallen leaves from the graves, and decorated them with sprigs of fresh willow. There was a reason for this. Willow was said to bring rain; putting it on the graves of ancestors was like a prayer for rain.

Offerings of food were set before the departed souls. The people prayed to them, imploring them to come and eat. When the souls of the ancestors had had time to eat the spiritual part of the food, the family feasted on the material part. This was not a sad day. Long ago it had been a day for dancing and making love. Later, ancestors were remembered with gladness on this day and everyone enjoyed a sumptuous picnic.

It was important to please the ancestors; their help would be needed if the earth was to bring forth an abundant harvest. To make doubly sure of their assistance, the seeds that were to be planted had been stored in the corner of the house where the spirits of the dead lived when they came to visit.

After the picnic people returned home. They lit new fires in their stoves in the ancient way, by rubbing two willow sticks together. Once more the making of fire marked a new beginning in the lives of men.

Branches of willow were hung on doors; girls and women stuck sprigs of willow in their hair. Everyone watched the sky for signs that meant a good harvest with plenty to eat for all. A rainbow was the best sign of all.

The Chinese harvest festival, Chung-Ch'iu, was the birthday of the moon. This was a very ancient festival. It took place on the fifteenth day of the Eighth Moon, the Harvest Moon. On that night the Queen of the Night, the moon, is at her brightest. The Chinese say that this is the only night of the year when the moon is perfectly round.

There were many legends about this festival, told in song and poetry. On this day thanks were given for the har-

Figure of Chinese moon goddess

vest. Cakes were baked, round as the moon. In the courtyard of each home an altar was set up. Five round plates were filled with round fruits arranged in a circle around a moon cake. Behind the altar there was often a scroll painted with a picture of the hare of the moon under a sacred cassia tree, from the leaves and bark of which the hare prepared a drug that was supposed to assure long life. (The leaves of the cassia tree are always green; it seems to live forever.)

At midnight, after a brief ceremony, the scroll was burned, so that the soul of the hare could return to the moon, its home. Each family then had a feast outdoors, under the moon. Farm people celebrated with roasted pigs, chickens, and fruit. Special pastries were offered to the Earth God as thanks for the harvest.

It was believed that beautiful flowers fell from the moon on this night. Women who saw the blossoms would have many children; men would be prosperous.

The holiday went on for three days, with music, and games and toys for the children.

Farmers in northern China and Korea finished their work in the fields by the end of September. They would not plant another crop of wheat until the spring. Farmers in central and southern China harvested rice in the fall but their task was not finished. Another crop was planted and the work continued. Still, for everyone Chung-Ch'iu meant that another year of seedtime and harvest had been completed, full circle, like the moon.

There were more festivals to come. The Feast of the Winter Solstice, like our Christmas, was a family festival. Candles and incense burned in the kitchen and everyone gathered there. On the table were ten pairs of red chopsticks and oranges with flowers stuck in them—peony for spring, lotus for summer, aster for autumn, and flowering almond for winter. At the feast, chairs were placed on the north side of the table for the ancestors who would eat the food spiritually before the family ate it in a worldly way.

The Chinese believed in sharing their food and happiness with growing things. After the feast the Chinese farmer would go out and feed the fruit trees by placing grains of rice in a notch of each tree.

The old ways change, but no one can change our dependence on the earth.

Japanese Rituals

MANY JAPANESE RICE farmers believe that a *kami,* or god, brings a plentiful harvest, though they themselves must plant the seed carefully and take good care of the fields. At the beginning of January the farmer makes an offering to the "year god." In his empty rice fields he sets out for the god a branch of pine or chestnut, or perhaps bamboo, with paper charms attached for good luck.

About the middle of January, before the first full moon, farmers in many Japanese villages gather one morning at a sacred rice field. There they act out every step in the growing of rice—planting the seeds, transplanting the seedlings to the flooded paddy fields, "chasing away the bird," and harvesting. If this is done well, the people say, there will be a good crop that year.

In early spring, before the rice fields are flooded, each farmer cuts a branch from a tree to represent the field god. This he sets up just where the god himself will enter the field along with the water that pours in to flood it. Carefully he places nearby a dish of freshly roasted rice seeds as an offering to this god.

There are separate ceremonies for all the stages in the growth of the rice crop. They vary from place to place. At one planting festival children sit in little boats that float on the water of a sacred rice field. There they beat drums while their elders on dry land stage a pantomime about the growing of rice.

Summer comes, and autumn with its harvest. First fruits are offered to the gods, and the people taste a sample of the new rice.

When at last the harvest is finished there is a gay festival in honor of the village god. He is sent back to the spirit world, where he will remain until the spring. The field god, who had entered the rice field with the water in the spring, is returned to the mountains, where he will be the mountain god until he is needed when the rice fields are flooded again.

Ceremonies such as these take place in the warm southern part of Japan, where rice is grown. To the north there are ceremonies for the growing of wheat and other foods. These are the rites of people who live on the land, close to nature every day of their lives.

All over Japan, in the cities and in the country, festivals are celebrated on important occasions. Some of these are related to the seasons; some are not.

The Japanese say good-bye to winter and welcome the approach of spring on Bean-Throwing Night, in early February. Bean-Throwing is an ancient ritual. Thousands of people go to temples and shrines to take part in the ceremony. In homes all over the country beans are thrown about as a symbol of spring sowing. It is thought that this will drive out the evil spirits of winter. People aim beans at dark corners of rooms where spirits may lurk. "Go out, devils!" they cry. "Come in, good luck!" There is one important rule, without which this bean-throwing could become chaotic: No one may throw more beans than the years of his age.

When the first day of spring has really come, on March 21, the Japanese celebrate with a Festival of Spring, which is a national holiday. This festival also has roots deep in the past when early people rejoiced because the long winter was over and green plants grew again in the earth. Special foods are offered to the ancestors and taken to neighbors as a springtime gift.

On October 17 there is a harvest festival, with dancing and laughter. The new grain is honored, and houses are decorated with the fruits of the earth.

Once again, in Japan as elsewhere in the world, the pattern of the year is completed.

14

Hindus, Moslems, and People of the Hills

THE PEOPLE OF INDIA FOLLOW MANY DIFFERENT RELIGIONS, all of which have their own rituals and their own festivals. The majority of the people, however, are Hindus. Like early people everywhere, the first Hindus worshiped the spirits of the natural world. There was a god of the sun, the rain, fire and wind, a sky father and earth mother. Hindus today still believe in many gods, though all are considered manifestations of one God.

Hindu festivals are numerous and they are often celebrated differently in different parts of the country. Some festivals celebrate the seasons. Others honor the sun, moon, and stars, the gods, or sacred plants and animals. Most have grown out of the ancient folklore and ritual of the people.

The Hindu year usually begins with the new moon just preceding the first day of spring (March 21 by our calendar). But spring itself is welcomed in northern and central

India with a festival called Holi, at the time of the full moon in the Hindu month of Phagun, usually in March. This is the gayest holiday of all.

Holi is one of the most ancient festivals in the world. It has its roots in the early worship of the sun that brings its welcome warmth to the earth in the springtime. On the eve of Holi, under the full moon, huge bonfires burn in towns and villages. Horns blow, drums beat, people make loud whoops as they beat their mouths with their hands.

The fires are sacred, and at first the people walk reverently around them. But then they let themselves go. They shout, they sing, they dance around the fires until dawn.

The fires may signify the burning of the old year to make way for the new. Loud noises are meant to scare away evil spirits that might try to interfere with the fertility of the earth, the animals, or even man himself.

At dawn water is poured on the fires to put them out. People dip their fingers in the ashes and make a mark on their foreheads, for good luck.

Then comes the exuberant day of Holi itself. People shower each other with crimson or saffron colored water. Boys squirt water from water pistols and bamboo blowpipes. Colored water is thrown from pans and pitchers. Scarlet powder is sprinkled about. People scream and run from the water—and enjoy it. Groups of revelers dance in the streets. All day long people eat sweets and other delicacies that have been prepared for this day. Necklaces of yellow and white sugar are given to children.

Holi has different names in different parts of India, and the customs vary. In some places it lasts three days, in others ten.

There are many legends to explain the colored water used at Holi. Here is one:

When the monkey god, Hanuman, was a small child he swallowed the sun. All the world was dark; no crops could grow. People were sad; they could find no way out of this disaster.

Then the gods ordered people to rub color on each other and laugh. Hanuman, with the sun still inside him, would watch. On the first day people tried to laugh but they were too sad. The next day they mixed water with colors and threw the bright mixture at each other with squeals of delight. Hanuman had never seen anything as funny as these hilarious people splashing color about and acting like silly clowns. Suddenly he gave one huge roaring laugh—and up came the sun.

For three days during the month of Bhadon, in late August or early September, Hindu women celebrate a festival for Gauri, goddess of the harvest and protector of women. A bundle of wild balsam wrapped in a silk cloth represents the goddess. On the first day an unmarried girl of a well-to-do family carries the bundle from room to room of her house. In each room women ask her, "What have you brought?" She answers, "Treasure to fill a city," or "Delicious food," or "Beautiful children," or some other phrase that is appropriate for that room. The women reply, "Come on golden feet, and stay forever." Each room will have good fortune.

The bundle representing Gauri is then offered milk and sweets, and girls sing before it. On the second day there is a feast.

On the third day a woman servant carries the bundle to a stream where she unwraps it and throws it into the water. She must bring back from the bank of the stream a handful of earth. This represents the rich soil beside the rivers where farmers first planted their gardens in early times.

There is a story told of Gauri. A poor Brahman (high-caste Hindu), sad because he was too poor to keep this festival, had an unexpected guest, an old woman. The woman blessed him with miraculous gifts of cows and food and told him to keep this festival each year for her. It was Gauri herself.

The old woman in the story means the departure of the old season at the time of the harvest. The young girl who carries the bundle of wild balsam in the festival represents the new season that is to come.

Some aspects of this festival may suggest to us other customs, in other places. The bundle of wild balsam recalls the bundle of grain that is sometimes still dressed up as the Corn Mother in parts of Europe. Long ago, you will remember, people threw images of the god Tammuz, or Adonis, into streams, as the bundle representing Gauri is thrown. Tammuz was drowned with weeping and wailing, but everyone knew he would come to life again. Gauri, too, will reappear when the crops have grown and been harvested another year.

Diwali is the name of five Hindu holidays that come all together at the end of October or beginning of November, usually at the end of the rainy season. This is a festival of lights. Hundreds of little clay saucers are filled with oil and a twisted cotton cord is placed in each one for a wick. On the first night of Diwali all the lamps are lit, on window-sills and on the edge of the flat roofs of houses, beside the roads, and on the banks of streams. Towns and cities glow with rows of softly flickering lights, like a dream world.

The lights are kept lit throughout Diwali, so that Lakshmi, the Hindu goddess of prosperity, can find her way to every home, coming silently on the wings of the Heavenly Owl.

As with most Hindu festivals, there are many versions of the origin of Diwali. In the north of India this is a harvest festival. The people believe that Lakshmi has spent the summer in the mountains. In the autumn she returns to the plains and the lowlands where most of the people live and grow their crops. She will need light to guide her to their homes.

In Allahabad, the City of God, on the Ganges River, young girls light their little lamps on the banks of the river and set them afloat. If her lamp reaches the opposite bank of the river with its wick still lighted, a girl is sure she will be married during the next year.

Each of the five days of Diwali also has its own name and its own meaning. The moon is honored. Sacred cows and bullocks are worshiped. This is the New Year of Business. In former times it was the New Year for all Hindus.

After the winter solstice, near the middle of January by our calendar, the Hindus have a three-day festival called Makara Sankranti. Everyone rejoices; days are growing longer and spring is on the way. There are feasts and family reunions. In the part of India called Bengal this festival also celebrates the harvesting of rice. People eat special rice cakes. Children wear necklaces of sugar birds which are fed to real birds on the following day.

During Makara Sankranti every Hindu who possibly can travels to the sacred river Ganges and bathes in its water. People believe that this sacred water will wash away all sin and evil. In Allahabad a great fair is held for the people. Those who cannot reach the Ganges bathe in other streams or rivers.

The Hindus are not the only people who believe in the purifying power of moving water. As we have seen, girls in parts of Europe wash their faces in a stream on Easter morning. On Midsummer Day women and girls used to bathe in a river; to them this meant a new beginning in their lives. Purification by water is a part of the ritual of many religions.

Rituals of the Saora People

IN THE mountains of India and in remote valleys live people who follow their own religion and celebrate their own festivals. These people may call themselves Hindus, but to most of them the Hindu gods seem far away. They worship first of all their own village gods or goddesses who can be counted on to help them when they are in need.

Among the people living in the hills of eastern India is a tribe known as the Saoras. Through thousands of years these people have kept their own customs, their own language, and their own religion.

The Saoras do not worship an earth mother; this is unusual. Various gods are thought by the Saoras to preside over the processes of agriculture. The people believe, too, that the spirits of the dead can interfere with the crops if they are not satisfied. These spirits demand a share of each harvest.

To the Saora every part of the growing of food is imbued with religion, from plowing to harvest. His field is a temple dedicated to the gods. There is a ceremony for each stage of the Saoras' work in the fields. The origin of all the ceremonies lies in the far distant past of the tribe.

In May comes the ceremony of blessing the seeds, Jammolpur, named for the god of seed, Jammolsum. First, in the morning, a special picture is painted by a priest. His paint is rice flour mixed with water, his brush a twig spread out at one end, his canvas the red clay wall of a house. The priest knows exactly what to paint; he has been told in a dream the night before.

The Saoras make these pictures for many purposes, often to please a god when a sacrifice is made to him, or to satisfy an ancestor who is thought to have brought trouble.

On the next page is a picture made for Labosum, god of the earth and the fields, at a Jammolpur ceremony. In the picture farmers are doing their work. Merrymakers dance around them, some waving their arms in the air, some carrying pots on their heads or their shoulders. A few carry two pots, in hope that the harvest will be twice as good as usual. Little birds, deer, and a porcupine are pictured; if they are honored in the picture, say the Saoras, surely they will not damage the growing plants in the fields. Sun and moon look down upon the scene.

Drawing by a Saora priest for Jammolpur

At the Jammolpur ceremony an altar is set up near the drawing a priest has made on the wall of one of the houses. Little baskets on the altar contain samples of the different kinds of seeds that are to be sown by the farmers of the village.

The priest begins to tell a tale of long-ago doings of men and gods. Once he breaks off the story long enough to kill a fowl and offer its blood to the gods. Scattering wine and seeds over the altar, he calls on the spirits of the ancestors.

The long tale of men and gods is then resumed. When it is finished leaf-cups containing rice and meat are put before the altar for the spirits. The chicken that was sacrificed has meanwhile been cooked, and the family feasts.

Each member of the family is given a little of the sacred seed from the altar to mix with the seed he is to sow. It should grow well.

When a crop is ready to harvest, no Saora will eat any of it until the proper ceremonies have been performed. The fruits of the earth are not his alone; they are given to everyone by the gods, who are the real owners of the fields. Offerings must be made to the gods before people can eat.

There are separate harvest festivals for some of the crops. The dates are not fixed; they depend on the weather and the decision of the priests.

Whatever the date, the harvest festivals are a delight to the hard-working Saora farmer and his family. Everyone is at his best. Girls wear flowers in their hair. Boys wind around their heads bright-colored turbans decorated with feathers. Shrines are adorned with leaves and the fruits of the earth.

Most important for the farmer is his feeling of satisfaction because he is doing what the gods require and doing it well. The gods are honored by being given the first fruits of the land. The dead are remembered at every shrine. Prayers for the future are offered and the people hope the gods will hear.

Together the people perform these rites and feel, once again, that they all face the future together, the living and the dead, human beings and gods. In the uncertain world of wind and weather, sun and rain, disease and disaster, this is a comfort to the people. It gives them courage.

One of the Saora harvest festivals is Rogonadur, for the red gram, a kind of bean. It takes place in December or January. A priest (or priestess) first makes an altar in his own house. Bunches of fresh gram are placed before it along with other food. The priest calls on the gods and the spirits of the ancestors to come and eat. He speaks like this:

"For you we sowed the seed, and now that the plants have grown and borne fruit we offer them first to you. . . . Be pleased with our sacrifice. . . . Spirits sitting on the trees, spirits sitting on the stones, spirits in caves and streams, . . . however many gods may be crowding the paths, push your way through and come! If there are great rivers in the way, make bridges over them and come. If there is a stream, throw a log of wood across it and come."

Speaking through the priest, representatives of the spirit world first scorn the offering, saying how small it is. Then, after long arguments, they are persuaded to accept it and give continued protection to the people.

The rest of the villagers hold their own festival of the red gram a week or more later. Bunches of freshly gathered beans are tied to roofs and pillars of the village shrines. Beans are offered to the ancestors in homes. Drummers visit each shrine and for four days there is ceremonial dancing. In the evening the people rejoice as they feast on rice and the new red gram.

At the end of the days of dancing there is a final rite to tell the gods to go away. The festival is finished and it is time for them to leave. Boys beat drums and gongs at a shrine, priests make a final offering of roast gram and then eat some themselves. This done, the drummers and the priest return home silently, so that the gods to whom they have said farewell will not follow them.

Moslem Rituals

THE RELIGION OF THE Moslems is called Islam. Moslems believe there is one God; Allah is his name and Mohammed is his Prophet. There are many people in India who follow this religion, and still more in Pakistan. There are Moslems also in other parts of Asia, in parts of Africa, and in eastern Europe. Each nation celebrates the Moslem holidays in its own way.

Islam is the youngest of the great religions of the world. Its holidays celebrate events in the life of Mohammed and Biblical characters whose stories are included in the sacred book of the Moslems, the Koran.

The Moslem calendar is based on the moon. Each month has 29½ days, taking in one waxing and waning of the moon. Since the Moslem year has 354 days, instead of the 365 of our solar calendar, the dates of holidays keep shifting, and they do not always come at the same season of the year. This calendar in itself makes a pattern of seasonal holidays almost impossible.

It is not surprising, in any case, that Moslem festivals are not related to the agricultural year. Many Moslems are not farming people and never have been. The Bedouins, Arabs of the desert in southwestern Asia and North Africa, most of them Moslems since the first days of Islam, have always been a wandering people, traveling from place to place with their camels, and sometimes with herds of goats and sheep. Only recently have some of them become farmers. Wandering Arabs never developed ceremonies and festivals for seedtime and harvest because these were not a part of their lives.

Other Moslems, however, have been and are farmers. As in Hindu India, Moslem people in remote valleys and mountains of other parts of Asia have kept some of their ancient customs. In Hunza, an almost inaccessible mountain area of Pakistan, the people call themselves Moslems but still perform some of the seasonal rituals which have been a part of their lives for countless years.

In the early spring the local ruler of Hunza, the Mir, puts on a magnificent gold-brocaded gown for the seed-sowing ritual. He carries his ceremonial sword in a carved ivory scabbard. Three times down the field and back the Mir drives a plow pulled by two oxen. Three times he sprinkles seed mixed with gold dust into the furrows he has plowed. Then he throws handfuls of the seeds into the air. Crowds have been watching, waiting for this moment. They push forward and reach eagerly for the seeds that have been thrown. If a farmer can catch even one seed and mix it with his own he is sure of an abundant wheat harvest.

So, too, farmers in Thailand reach for a handful of seed that has been blessed and thrown in the air. And in the hills of India Saoras mix sacred seeds with their own before they plant.

Some Moslems have a ceremony toward the end of their year in which they wail and lament loudly the death, fifty years after that of Mohammed, of his grandson Husain, who was killed in battle and is considered a martyr. The story of Husain is told in great detail at wooden pulpits in the streets, while the people cry "O Husain, O Husain!" with groans and tears. After nine days of this, a procession acts out the burial of Husain. Horses and men march behind his coffin; one horse represents Duldul, Husain's battle horse. At the end of the procession some fifty men beat wooden staves together in a steady rhythm.

In more recent years a play of forty to fifty scenes about Husain has been given on the tenth day. The excitement at this play is so great that spectators sometimes try to lynch the actors who represent the murderers of Husain.

The festival for Husain originated in Mesopotamia, the "land between the rivers." This is where, in ancient times, the death of Tammuz was remembered each year with prolonged wailing. Tammuz was a god of vegetation. The Moslems wail for Husain, a hero who had nothing to do with vegetation at all, but this is nevertheless their version of the ancient ceremony.

Also in Pakistan, a largely Moslem country, young men and boys welcome spring with a wild kite-flying contest. Graceful bright-colored kites dance in the wind. The string of each kite has been stiffened with starch or glue and made sharp with powdered glass. The trick is for a player to get his string to cross the string of another kite, rub against it, and cut the kite down. The other kite falls to earth, a battered heap of bright paper and bamboo.

It is hard to keep a kite up in a sky full of other kites without getting it tangled in the trees or cut down. Men and boys climb up on the flat roofs of the houses and sometimes, as they reach for the sky, they fall off.

In Iran, west of India and Pakistan, the most important holiday is No-ruz, which means "New Day." This marks the beginning of a new year in the solar calendar followed by the Iranians. It is also the first day of spring, March 21. Both Moslems and non-Moslems celebrate No-ruz. Moslems include a reading of the Koran at home, while everyone munches delicious candy.

Iran is a part of Mesopotamia. It is a dry country, swept by cold winds in the winter, intensely hot in the summer. But rains come with springtime and for a time the world is green with fresh leaves and bright with flowers. To Iranians this seems indeed the beginning of a new year.

On No-ruz, at the very moment when the new year begins, between the dusk and darkness of New Year's Eve, each family is sitting at home around a clean tablecloth spread on the floor. There are seven kinds of food on the cloth, a lighted candle, and a green leaf for every member of the family. (The leaf signifies new life and growth.)

Live goldfish swim in a bowl on the cloth; they are said to stay still for a moment at the turn of the year. An orange in a pot of water is believed to revolve just then.

An Iranian legend says that the earth trembles when a new year begins. At the family gathering, an egg is placed on a mirror. At the right moment it trembles a little! (Perhaps the egg trembles because cannons are shot off to welcome the new year.) People shout with joy, kiss, and congratulate one another.

There is another interesting custom connected with the

Iranian New Year. About two weeks before No-ruz seeds of wheat, celery, or lentil are scattered in a bowl of water. When they have sprouted they are placed in dishes or clay jugs containing earth and put in the sunlight. The plants are watered well and they rapidly send up green shoots. On the twelfth and last day of the No-ruz celebration the jug with its green plants is thrown over the garden wall or into a stream. This is said to mean that quarrels are thrown away and the new year begins in peace.

These jugs of growing greenness may have still another meaning, however. They recall the "Gardens of Adonis" of ancient times, shallow baskets or pots in which little "gardens" were grown and then cast into the sea or into springs, along with images of the dead god Adonis. This was done in memory of the god of vegetation who was said to bring the green plants to the earth each year when he came to life again. In a similar way, in Iran today, dishes or jugs of growing plants are thrown over the garden wall or into a stream when springtime has made the world green once more. Old customs change; often they do not die.

15

South America, Past and Present

MANY AMAZING CIVILIZATIONS EXISTED IN SOUTH AMERICA IN early and ancient times. Very little is known about them because the people left no written records. Not one of these civilizations developed writing.

The Indians called Incas had no writing, either, but we know a good deal about their culture because other people wrote about it. The Inca Empire stretched over two thousand miles along the Pacific coast of South America and up into the Andes Mountains, covering present-day Peru and parts of neighboring countries. It flourished during the period of time which in Europe was called the Middle Ages, and into modern times. (The Middle Ages lasted for about a thousand years, from the fall of the Roman Empire to modern times.)

The Incas were conquered by a band of Spaniards from Europe in the sixteenth century, more than four hundred years ago, and it was some of these Spaniards who wrote the first accounts of these people.

The Incas worshiped the Sun. They believed that their king was descended from the Sun and was himself divine. When he moved among the people he was the earthly representative of the Sun passing among the stars.

There were other Inca gods, too. The earth mother, Pachamama, was worshiped by the farming people, who knew her worth. They also worshiped the moon.

Most of the Incas, in fact, were farmers. For them there was no separation between religion and daily life. The growing of food in the earth was a religious act and everything connected with it was holy. All of life was controlled by unseen powers which were present in mountains, rivers, lakes, and even in the boundary stones at the edge of a planted field. The Indian must please these powers in order to live at peace with them.

The Incas lived south of the equator, where the seasons are the reverse of ours. Summer there comes during our winter, although, as in tropical Africa, there is no real summer or winter near the equator. In the part of the Andes Mountains where the Incas lived, the rainy season begins in October. Winter months, from June to October, are dry.

The climate varies with the height of the land. Deep valleys are hot all year round. In the mountains nights are cool and days are warm.

The calendar of the Incas had twelve months, each named for a festival that took place in that month. There was a festival for every important step in the growing of maize (which we call corn), the principal crop.

The first month of the Inca year was Kapaj Raymi, at the time of our December. Kapaj Raymi was called the

Great Festival. The land had been plowed several months before, the maize had been planted, all the proper rituals had been accomplished, and the people waited for the first shoots of green to appear in the fields.

The rainy season had begun and it was important to see that the rains behaved. If they ceased too soon, the maize would not grow. On the other hand, if heavy rains poured down the mountains in floods, the tender young plants would wash away. So the Kapaj Raymi was devoted to the storm god.

The succeeding months, named for their festivals, were called "The small ripening," "The great ripening," "The garment of flowers," "The dance of the young maize." In our month of May, autumn in South America, the people joined together in the fields for the "Song of the harvest." First fruits were offered to the gods at the shrines in the fields.

The great Festival of the Sun was held in June, at the time of the winter solstice. From that time on the sun's path in the sky would be a little higher each day. For three days before the festival no fires were lighted in the capital city, Cuzco. Everyone fasted.

The Inca, the Sun King himself, spent the night before the solstice alone in the great stone hall of the Temple of the Sun. There he welcomed the sun at dawn as it shone on the golden wall within the temple. As the sun burst in, the Inca put on his headdress and sandals and prepared to lead a procession of all the people of Cuzco.

New fire was lit directly from the sun itself, by concentrating its beams on a concave plate and reflecting them onto soft cotton. A pure white llama was offered to the sun

Figure of an Inca offering maize

and burned in this fire. Sheep and lambs for the feast were roasted in it. New fire was taken to the Temple of the Sun, where the holy flame would be kept burning all through the year.

July was the time of clearing the land in preparation for the next year's harvest. August was plowing time. In Cuzco the Inca himself broke the earth for the first time each year with the stab of a golden digging stick. Everywhere, throughout the lands of the Inca, officials of the government did the same. Then the men, in long lines across the fields, loosened the earth with their own digging sticks, singing songs like this:

> Ho, Victory, Ho! Victory,
> Here digging stick, here the furrow!
> Here the sweat, here the toil!

Women followed, breaking up the loosened clods of earth with a kind of hoe. The earth mother, Pachamama, had come alive.

This was a gay festival. On plowing day people wore their best clothes and put flowers in their hair.

The growing of maize was in itself a kind of festival. People worked together, singing, on all the fields. But the special festivals were a welcome change from the daily routine. There were sometimes as many as ten joyful days of processions, singing, and dancing. Everyone played a part.

The growing of crops concerned not only the people but the gods; rituals asked their help or gave thanks for help already received. Each ritual had to be carefully performed. The farmers were convinced that if this was not done the seeds would not sprout in the earth, rains would fail or floods might wash away the young plants.

After Christianity had been brought to the Incas, the Christian God was sometimes identified with the Sun God of former times. The earth mother, Pachamama, became the Virgin Mary.

High in the Andes, in Cuzco, people today hold a week-long ceremony in which they salute the sun and sing chants in its honor. A llama is sacrificed to the sun. Then everyone dances. This is now partly a Christian ceremony, but it has its roots in the Incas' age-old festival to the Sun God.

The harvest festival of the Incas, Aymuray, has been replaced by the Christian Feast of the Invention of the Cross, held on May third. The Aymuray was a nighttime festival in honor of long winter nights to come and the life-giving powers sent from the starry skies to make the earth fertile.

Today the eve of the Invention of the Cross is a mixture of Christian and Inca customs. It is a merry holiday night. All along the highways, and on mountains where there are crosses, bonfires burn. In towns and villages altars are set up, with a lighted cross in the background, trimmed with bright-colored ornaments and flowers. By the roadsides, in the chill of the night, the Indians make merry with guitars and flutes. There are jugs of the drinks the Indians enjoy.

Next day crosses are carried in procession to the nearest church, where a mass is said for them.

There are still some five million Quechuas, people of the Incas, most of them in Peru. Many of their customs are unchanged. Their traditional religion is still mixed with their ideas of Christianity.

Many different kinds of people live in South America, with varying levels of civilization. In the warm jungles along the Amazon River and its tributaries live tribes of primitive Indians whose way of life has changed very little for thousands of years. With only the simplest tools and the hostile jungle all around them, these Indians occupy most of their time with the daily business of survival.

They hunt and fish with bow and arrow and gather fruits from the jungle. Most of them also plant gardens in which they grow mostly manioc, a plant whose starchy roots are processed and made into a kind of pancake. In some places maize is grown, and various vegetables.

Customs vary from tribe to tribe. There is no overall pattern of ritual for planting and harvest. Some tribes do not hold ceremonies for the whole community at all. And our knowledge of many of these people is still limited.

The men of one tribe in the Brazilian wilderness perform an impressive dance designed to bring the rain and make the fruits of the forest flourish. Their heads are adorned with crowns of bright feathers. Arms and shoulders are covered with leaves, to look like trees. Bending their heads, the men dance about, waving their leafy arms gently in time with the music of two musicians. One of these shakes a rattle, the other beats the ground with a large gourd, imitating thunder.

This dance alone should be sufficient to ensure the fruitfulness of the forest. But if the spirits seem contrary, a bull-roarer is added to the ceremony. This Indian bull-roarer is a slat in the shape of a fish, decorated with red zigzag or diamond designs. No spirit can resist the frightening whirr it makes when it is twirled. It is strong magic here in Brazil, as it is with many primitive people in other parts of the world.

Some tribes dance to the music of sacred flutes and trumpets. Without this, they believe, the fruits and berries in the forest will not grow. Bamboo flutes are also played by certain tribes in sacred ceremonies when they plant their gardens.

Of course, not all the Indians of South America are as primitive as those of the Amazon jungle. We have seen that descendants of the Incas still live in Peru, retaining many of their age-old customs in spite of contact with Christianity and European civilization. Some Indians have kept intact not only their ancient customs but their religion. Among these are the Mapuche Indians in Chile.

To the Mapuches nothing is more important than the spirits of their ancestors. People who follow the rules of

Mapuche society in their lifetimes become after death "hawks of the sun," ancestral spirits who help the living and influence everything they do.

The Mapuches are farmers. Their principal ceremony lasts for at least two days, before the ripening of the grain or after the harvest. The date is set by important people of the community, but it is always at about the time of a full moon.

The ceremony is held on a special field that has an altar at each end. Each day begins with an early morning prayer by a ritual priest to ñenechen, the Supreme Being, and to the ancestors. Then men on horseback gallop counterclockwise around the field, circling the two altars, whooping to drive away evil spirits. Some may wear sheepskin masks to frighten away ghosts.

Men and women dance around one of the altars, wildly at first, then slowly. All wear sprigs of wheat and barley, or kernels of maize, which they have plucked from the decorations on the altar. These trimmings from the altar are sacred and the people feel they are holy while they wear them.

Beside the field men blow whistles made of clay or wood or stone. Someone toots on a long trumpet. There is a continual beating of drums. All this is the music for the dance.

Four separate times the priest prays. Between the prayers long lines of men and women dance in place. At one point a sheep is killed by the priest, with a prayer to ñenechen and the hawks of the sun. The priest cuts out the bloody heart of the sheep and places it in the forked stick of the main altar. He sprinkles the sheep's blood on the altar and on the fire that burns near it. The sheep itself is burned. All this is the sacrifice. If the people have few animals, however, they may roast the sheep instead and have a ritual feast.

After another prayer the priest scatters seeds of grain about, asking ñenechen and the hawks of the sun to send abundant harvests to the people.

Again, everyone dances.

The same general pattern of ritual is repeated four times during the day, and again on the second day.

The Mapuche Indians farm on poor soil, planting poor seed. Everything they grow may be ruined by heavy rains and summer winds. But they keep trying. This is the way they have always lived. Every year they ask the blessing of ñenechen and the hawks of the sun. Who else will help them, the Mapuches ask. Who else has given them what little they already have?

Most of the people in South America are Roman Catholics and their festivals are those of the Christian Church. Since the seasons south of the equator are the opposite of those to the north, the *fiestas* of the church are often not related to the seasons. Christmas, for example, is a winter holiday in Europe. But though the date remained the same when it was exported to South America, it is a summer festival there. Easter comes in the autumn.

The Indians, as we have seen, combine Christianity with their native religion. Those who live on the land have not forgotten that their lives depend on the sun and the rain, the plants that grow in the earth and the animals that live on it.

In the village of Hualcan, in the mountains of Peru, for example, the major fiestas still come at times of importance in the growing of crops. A festival in October honors Saint Ursula, who is the patron saint of the village, looking after the health of the people and their harvests from the fields. October is the beginning of the planting season in Hualcan, just before the summer rains. It is a good time for the Indians to ask divine help for their fields. (The Incas held their Festival of Water at this time.)

Carnival comes just before Lent, after the planting season is over and the plants have begun to grow. Crosses are put up in sacred locations, to protect both the people and the fields against evil.

Carnival is the most popular festival in all of South America. In Europe it was a celebration of the approaching spring. In South America it has completely lost this meaning, for there Carnival takes place in the summer.

In Brazil the three days of Carnival are presided over by the mythical Momus, ancient Greek god of mockery. It used to be the custom to bury Momus on the last day. In the cities people gathered in theaters and conducted a mock-solemn funeral service, interrupted every now and then by thousands of people singing the gay tunes they had sung on the streets during the three days of Carnival. In earlier times in Europe this ceremony would have meant the burial of winter.

Today the songs are the most popular part of Carnival. People everywhere make up new ones or adapt old ones. In Rio de Janeiro, capital of Brazil, there is a contest to select the best songs.

On the last day a procession of floats moves through the streets of Rio, each portraying an important event of the preceding year. Everyone turns out to watch, still gay, still singing.

Then Carnival is over and life returns to normal.

Easter comes at the time when the first ripe vegetables are gathered. This is not like the rebirth of the earth in our own springtime, but it is a sign that the fruits of the earth have ripened again and life will go on. As everywhere, Easter is a time to rejoice, and there is a fiesta to celebrate it.

The Indian fiesta is a time of wild excitement. A mass is held in the church, and there is a religious procession, but the rest of the time is taken up with fireworks, eating, drinking, and dancing to the music of such instruments as guitar, harp, and drum. Men wear bright-edged shawls over their shoulders; women put on long woolen skirts. Both day and night are filled with noise and hilarity; no one gets much sleep. There are markets with many things to buy and sell. The monotonous rhythm of the daily routine is broken and everyone is refreshed.

The old pagan custom of lighting fires on Midsummer Eve has been carried across the ocean to South America, as a part of the Saint John's Day festival on June 24 (winter in South America). In Brazil, people jump over the fires of Saint John. In Bolivia bonfires are lighted in the streets of the capital city, La Paz, and fires burn on the steep hills around the city. Indians climb far up on the heights to light their fires. The city, deep in a valley, seems surrounded by bursts of bright light that flicker in the darkness.

South America is a varied continent, from high cold mountains to steaming hot jungles. The rites of the people are varied, too, from dancing in crowns of bright feathers in the wilderness to singing while a Carnival procession winds through city streets.

16

The Aztecs Celebrated Maize

IN 1519, TWENTY-SEVEN YEARS AFTER COLUMBUS DISCOVERED America, the Spanish explorer Cortez landed on the shores of Mexico with about six hundred soldiers. Within two years Cortez and his men had conquered the Aztecs, Indians who then controlled most of Mexico. The land became a Spanish province and remained one until Mexico gained its independence about three hundred years later.

Unlike the Incas of South America, the Aztecs did have writing, made up of stylized pictures and certain abstract signs. Unfortunately most of the examples of Aztec writing were destroyed by the Spaniards. As with the Incas, we must rely on the accounts of Spanish and later historians for our knowledge of these people.

The Aztecs were warriors, merchants, and farmers. Some were master craftsmen. Weapons of war were beautifully decorated. Elaborate paintings and maps were done in color on sheets of parchment, paper made from fiber, and cloth.

Religion influenced every aspect of the lives of the Aztecs. The farmer thought of the earth as a goddess; none of it could be owned by a mere human. Instead, chiefs of government agencies parceled out different pieces of land for the use of the people every year. The farmer accepted with gladness his share of Mother Earth. Most of the families grew their own food. As with the Incas, maize was of first importance.

The Aztecs knew that they could not control nature. Their lives depended on the sun in the sky, the gentle rains that watered their crops, the hail that sometimes destroyed them, the droughts that dried up the earth.

The gods were everywhere, sending the rain and the sunshine. There were spirits of growth in all the plants; so it seemed logical to the Aztecs to make offerings to the spirits of the maize.

The Aztecs believed in a Supreme Deity, Ome Tecuhtli. He was the Lord of Life, above all other gods. He gave a soul to each human child, but no one had any direct experience of this god.

Mother Earth, Coatlicue, was a goddess who was treated with special reverence. She was the mother of animals, wild plants, and all the food grown by man. But no one could be sure of her. She brought forth food from the earth, but she could also cause earthquakes and bring famine.

There were countless little spirits everywhere, in flowers and springs of water, in trees and rocks and mountains. These were the daily companions of the people.

The gods gave life to man. The Aztecs felt that they must, in return, offer to the gods this same gift, human life. Over and over again they sacrificed human beings, often warriors who had been captured in battle, sometimes women and children.

This seems to us a horrible and needless practice, but the Aztecs were convinced that without it the sun would not cross the sky each day and their lives on earth could not continue.

The victim of sacrifice was not pitied. He was to carry messages from the people to the gods and was assured of a happy future in heaven. If he was a captured warrior his spirit would become one of the eagles who lifted the sun from the darkness of night and brought it out into the morning light. The sudden pain of the knife that caused death was considered preferable to wounds and illness and old age.

The climate of Mexico is generally mild. There, too, summer does not differ widely in temperature from winter. The dry season, from about October through April, is followed by the rainy season, May through September. (This does not mean that it rains all the time.) There is more rain in some sections than in others.

As in other warm parts of the world, the climate varies with altitude. Valleys may be steaming hot; high land may have perpetual spring. The heart of Mexico is a high tableland ringed with mountains. The Aztec capital, Tenochtitlan, now Mexico City, is in a great valley on this tableland.

The Aztecs divided their agricultural year into eighteen periods of twenty days each, with a leftover period of five unlucky days at the end of the year during which everyone stayed at home and did as little as possible. Each twenty-day period began with a festival and feast for a particular god.

Aztec ceremonies were full of mystery and color. The

priest dressed in the elaborate costume of the god being honored. The shrine was decorated with flowers and perfumed with incense. Dancers moved to the rhythm of flutes, whistles, rattles, bells, and drums.

The pattern of festivals followed the growth of the maize in a general way, but it was very complicated. Some festivals honored more than one god. Some do not seem to us today to belong in the agricultural year, but all were a part of the Aztec's experience with the gods who controlled his life on the earth.

The maize plant was loved by the people. It gave them so much in return for their care and their ceremonies to the gods. Some of the monthly festivals related directly to its growth.

The festival of Xipe Totec, god of newly planted seed, took place on February 22 by our calendar, before the maize was sown. If they did not honor the god, the Aztecs were sure that their seeds would not sprout and grow.

The maize seed died each year and was buried until green shoots broke through the old skin and lifted themselves into the light. The people, too, felt that their lives were renewed at this time. All this was possible because the god

Head of maize god

Xipe Totec had long ago given food to mankind by having himself skinned alive, just as the maize seed loses its skin. Prisoners of war were sacrificed at this festival.

On April 3 the god of the tender young maize plant, Cinteotl, was honored. People offered the god their own blood. This song was sung:

> Born is the Maize-god
> In the House of Descent,
> In the place where the flowers are,
> The god One-flower.
>
> The Maize-god is born
> In the place of water and mist
> Where the children of man are made,
> In beautiful Michoacan.

The lovely goddess of the growing maize, Xilonen, was honored in a grand festival which began on June 22. A slave girl represented the goddess. (In Europe she might have been called the Corn Mother.) Her face was painted half red, half yellow, and she wore a crown of cardboard with bright green plumes waving on top, like tassels of the maize. Her collar was made of green precious stones, and her dress was red, "the color of spring flowers," the Aztecs said. Day after day she danced until at last, after the eighth and last day of the festival, she was sacrificed to the goddess.

Meanwhile girls had danced in procession each night, taking samples of new green maize to the temples. They all wore their hair loose down their backs, so the maize would grow just as luxuriantly. Their loosened hair showed, too, that they were little girls not yet ready for marriage.

A festival for "our grandmother," Tosi, a form of the mother of the gods, Coatlicue, was held toward the end of the summer, beginning with a week of dancing accompanied by a two-toned gong. Tosi was also goddess of the ripe maize. Girls wrapped up bundles of the sacred first fruits of this harvest and carried them on their backs, as if they were their own babies. For the moment they became the spirit of the maize, carrying its newborn life to the temple. Priests blessed the maize cobs, and the girls raced home to put them in a special bin above the huge baskets where the rest of the maize was stored. During the coming year the blessed cobs would preserve the life in the rest of the maize which was food for the family.

The many Aztec festivals connected with rain honored the various aspects of life on the earth. Tlaloc, father of all the rain gods, lived on the mountaintops where clouds gather. The rain gods were of great importance, because without rain nothing could grow.

The first period of the agricultural year began on February second with a festival for rain. The priest who represented Tlaloc, "he who makes things grow," wore a headdress of white heron feathers, soft as the clouds that promised rain. His mask was painted blue, the color of water against the sky. His face and body were painted black, like the storm clouds.

In March, after another festival to the rain gods, the first fruits of the year, especially flowers, were offered to the gods. No one would think of smelling a flower until the offerings had been made. Temples and shrines were decorated with new green stalks of maize.

An autumn festival honored all the high mountains where the rain clouds gather. People made models of mountains out of a special dough. In November they took vows to make images of the mountain gods so that the mountains would become the home of the rain. Then clouds would gather around them and pour down their water.

The rain god Tlaloc has not been without influence in recent times. In the fall of 1968 exuberant students in Mexico City climbed up a statue of Tlaloc and sat on its head. This was an insult to the rain god, some people said. It was most unwise. The god could make rain fall on the Olympic Games, scheduled for October in Mexico City. And in fact it poured during the games, more than once. But the contests went on just the same. Dripping athletes ran races in the rain.

At the heart of all Aztec worship was the fire god, Xiuhtecuhtli, a symbol of the Supreme Creator. In a summer festival slaves were sacrificed to the god by being thrown into a fire. In addition to this grim ceremony there was a merry contest in which young people climbed a greased pole to win prizes.

The last festival of the year was also devoted to the god of fire. He was represented at different times by two priests dressed in appropriate costumes. One wore bright green quetzal feathers and a mask of blue and green stones. He was fire as a god of growing plants. The other represented the god as burning fire. He dressed in red feathers of the macaw and wore a mask of red and black stones.

All the fires in the temples and in the houses of the people were put out at this festival. The priests made new fire by rubbing two sticks together before an image of the god.

Other Indians in Mexico, especially in the southern part, kept many of the customs that had belonged to them for countless years. At harvest time the Zapotecs walked in procession to their fields of maize, where they picked out the largest and finest sheaf they could find. This sheaf was placed, with great ceremony, on an altar brightly decorated with wild flowers, after which it was wrapped in fine linen and kept by the priests until planting time. The sheaf was then carried back to the field in procession and buried, still wrapped in linen, in a special place underground. Maize was sown, and when the time for harvest came again, the buried sheaf was dug up and its kernels of maize were given by the priests to all who asked. The buried sheaf was thought to make the maize grow well.

These ceremonies were still being celebrated each year long after the Spanish conquest.

One ceremony that is still performed today is the rain dance of the Totonac Indians who live near Veracruz on Mexico's east coast. Four men do this dance. They climb a ninety-foot ceremonial pole, wind ropes around its top, and attach the loose ends of the ropes to their ankles. At a signal the dancers suddenly leap outward, head first, with arms outspread. Quickly the ropes unwind, and the men spin around the pole, swinging in wider and wider circles until they reach the ground.

In about two minutes, as he descends, each man makes thirteen turns around the pole. The four men make a total of fifty-two turns, one for each week in the year. Each dancer

Zapotec maize god

represents a season of the year—spring, summer, autumn, winter. The Indians say that the dance has never failed to bring rain.

As the Indian "raindrops" fall, a Totonac priest, on a platform at the top of the pole, chants: "Mother Earth is everything. Mother Earth is life and death. Without rain there is no life."

In 1960, when Mexico celebrated 150 years of freedom, this ceremony was made a part of the festivities, at the request of the Mexican government. It is more than a thousand years old. Originally the four men were dressed as macaws, birds sacred to the sun. Their descent from the pole was a kind of religious game, called the Volador.

The Spaniards brought Christianity to Mexico and most of the people are now Catholics. As in South America, the Indians have often mixed their old beliefs with Christianity. The great Mexican celebration now is the fiesta. This may be a saint's day, anniversary of a historical event in the Christian Church, Carnival, festival of the dead (Halloween), Christmas, or just a local affair. The fiesta is the Indian's time to relax and have fun; he does it with abandon.

At a typical fiesta church bells start ringing at midnight and keep ringing until dawn. Dancers perform in the town square, wearing plumed headdresses and masks, to the music of guitars, piccolos, and violins. Merry-go-rounds and bands are for the amusement of everyone. There is a market where handicrafts are bought and sold—pottery, baskets, embroidery, glassware, and such, along with food and other necessities.

After sundown there is a solemn procession into the church with lanterns, and then more dancing. Fireworks boom and crackle. Pinwheels and rockets trace bright designs across the sky.

Though some customs remain, the Aztec pattern of festivals has gone, and along with it the horror of human beings sacrificed to the gods. But the Indians of Mexico have not forgotten that "Mother Earth is everything. Mother Earth is life and death."

17

Ceremonies of the North American Indians

MANY TRIBES OF INDIANS LIVED NORTH OF MEXICO BEFORE the white man came to North America. Some lived by hunting wild animals and by gathering nuts, seeds, and roots. Some planted gardens. Others lived by both hunting and planting; the men hunted and the women took care of the gardens.

As with the Indians farther south, maize was the most important crop. Corn is the usual word for maize in this part of North America, and we will call it corn in this chapter.

The customs of the Indian tribes of North America varied greatly, according to the kind of land they lived on, the climate, and their own inclinations. Their religion varied, too, but a few beliefs were shared by all. Like most primitive people, these Indians believed that spirits were everywhere in nature. (By primitive people we mean those who live as early people did.) Some Indians believed that there was a Great Spirit over all, unseen but powerful, but there was no general agreement about the nature of this spirit.

Religion was a part of everything the Indian did, including his daily search for food. But it was through ceremonies that the Indian made personal contact with the spirits. He knew that these spirits could bring disaster to man as well as good fortune. It was wise to perform the rituals carefully, following patterns established by the spirits themselves at the beginning of the world. Then the rhythm of man's world would continue, as it always had.

The Indian felt that he had a kind of partnership with the spirits. Both of them benefited from the ceremonies; both could feel at peace when a ceremony was completed, because then all was well.

Indian ceremonies changed somewhat after the white man came. They became more colorful. Before that time the Indians had no scarlet cloth, no bright-colored beads. Feathers were mostly gray or brown, with an occasional red from the head of a woodpecker. Paints were of delicate colors, made of such natural materials as roots and berries.

Color did not matter, however. The important thing in a ceremony was *movement,* and this meant the dance. Dances were intended to get across an idea to the spirits; no dance was performed for the pleasure of an audience. Sound accompanied all the movements—a constant beating of drums and shaking of rattles. Songs, too; these were part of the message.

The Zuni sometimes sang of:

> . . . striped cloud wings
> and massed cloud tails
> of all the birds of summer.

Hunters and food gatherers had few ceremonies. Hunting was lonely work and group life consisted of an occasional roaring feast. Each individual had his own personal relationship with the spirits.

The farming Indians, on the other hand, settled in groups with their fields around them, mostly in eastern North America and in some places west of the Mississippi River. Together, in families or in larger groups, they broke the ground, planted their seeds, and reaped the harvest. The rain and the sunshine were matters of concern to the whole community. Ceremonies were repeated over and over again, year after year, and in time they acquired a definite pattern. Dates were set to correspond with the growth of the plants. Priests learned the long rituals and presided over the ceremonies.

Mother Earth was held in reverence, but she was not the great mother-goddess of ancient times in Europe and western Asia, bringing life to the earth each spring. There were no special ceremonies for her. The American Indian Mother Earth was a kindly producer of food. The Navahos believed that she was young when the corn was young and grew older as the seasons progressed.

This Mother Earth demanded no sacrifice. Even animals were seldom sacrificed to the spirits in North America. The Indians did make certain offerings, such as tobacco or corn meal, as a kind of reminder that spirits and men had an agreement about the way of the world.

The sun was considered the actual source of life by the Indian farmers. Fire was the sun's representative here on earth. Both life and death on earth depended on the sun, especially when the year turned toward winter or summer. Ceremonies were needed to help him.

Lesser spirits had their place in ceremonies, too—the winds, sometimes the stars.

We will consider a few of the ceremonies of these planting Indians in this chapter, mostly as they took place before the coming of the white man changed Indian life.

The Natchez Indians lived in the forest in the southern part of the United States, near the present city of Natchez, Mississippi. Like the Incas farther south, the Natchez worshiped the sun and believed that their ruler was descended from him. Sometimes they sacrificed a prisoner of war to the sun, but they did not approach the number of executions carried out by the Aztecs.

Corn and other crops were grown in fields on which the trees had been cut down or burned away. Every summer the Natchez held a first-fruits ceremony. No one was allowed to touch the ripe ears of corn in his own field until this ceremony was finished.

The warriors of the tribe cultivated a special field for the ceremony. There the people, led by their chief, the Sun, lived in temporary cabins and cooked and ate the sacred corn from the field. New fire was made by the ancient method of twirling a stick, and this lit the cooking fires of each family.

It was several days before all the corn was finished. Meanwhile the men amused themselves in various ways. Sometimes they played with a ball made of deerskin stuffed with moss. The game involved hitting the ball with the hands, never holding it or letting it fall, until it was whacked against the cabin of one's own side.

The Cherokee Indians also lived in the forest, in what is

Maize (corn)

now eastern Tennessee and western North Carolina. They celebrated each stage of the growth of the corn with a ceremony.

According to a Cherokee myth, the corn sprang from the blood of an old woman who was killed by her disobedient sons. Each year, when the crop was nearly ready, a Cherokee priest holding a rattle would sit in a small hut in the center of a field of corn and sing songs, calling on the Old Woman, spirit of the corn. Before long the priest and his assistant would hear a loud rustling outside the hut; the Old Woman was bringing the corn into the field! They must not look up, however, until the song was finished. They never saw the Old Woman; she was gone before they looked.

This ceremony was repeated for four nights. No one went near the field for seven nights after that. The priest went then. If the ritual had been performed properly he would find young ears of corn on the stalks.

The Iroquois Indians believed that the Spirit of the Corn was three sisters dressed in leaves of the corn plant. The sisters were very fond of one another and were delighted to be together. There was a story that long ago the corn had produced its ears more abundantly, until an evil spirit went into the fields and took away some of its fruitfulness. When the wind rustled in the corn, the Indians heard the Spirit of the Corn weeping for its lost abundance.

The Iroquois lived on the fertile land that is now the central part of New York State. They believed that since new human life comes from the body of a woman, the corn, too, needed her care if it was to be fruitful. So the women did most of the work in the fields. Women also danced to make the corn grow, or the beans or squash, while the men sang.

There were ceremonies throughout the year of the Iroquois. The longest and most important was the New Year ceremony, held in late January or early February, during the second moon after the winter solstice. This was the time when the Creator might bring the springtime back to the earth, or his enemy might prevent him from doing so. The people could help by purifying themselves.

Sitting in a longhouse, led by a priest, each Indian told all the wrong things he had done since the last confession. Then old fires were put out on every hearth and the ashes scattered. Priests lit new fires.

After that, people told the dreams they had dreamed about the troubles and problems they had experienced during the year just past. It was good to speak of these things; everyone felt better when it was done.

More ritual followed. People acted out the mythical gambling contest in which the Creator had won springtime and green growth and all other good things from the forces of evil.

In the afternoon there were dances and games. "The people now upon the earth" were to be given new life by this festival. It was a gay time, and the people needed it. The crops had been harvested long since, fall hunting and fishing were finished, and everyone had been confined in crowded houses throughout the cold weather. The festival was a change —both solemn ritual and fun and laughter. Everyone could let go and relax.

Another important Iroquois rite was the Drum Dance of Thanksgiving. Every ceremony began with a short version of this dance. Thanks were given to the earth, "our mother who supports our feet," and to the grasses, plants, trees, birds, animals, the three-sister spirits of the corn, and so on, through wind, sun, moon, and stars to the Creator himself. This catalogue of blessings was interrupted now and then by a whoop, the sound of the water drum, and a song.

The Indians then offered tobacco to the spirits. It was placed in the fire as incense, so its smoke could carry prayers to the Creator.

A long version of the Drum Dance took place during the Green Corn Moon (or month), in August. This ceremony is now a part of an annual Iroquois pageant which is intended to help white people understand the ways of the Indian.

The Indians who lived in the vicinity of the Great Lakes, and those on the prairie, had still other ceremonies. Many of these Indians were both hunters and planters. Some, at their planting and harvest ceremonies, asked of the Great Spirit not rain or abundant crops but, first of all, success in war.

The Pawnees on the prairie believed that corn came to the world as a woman, Mother Corn. Some said that she was also the mother of men. They believed also in a Supreme Being who was father of all things on earth. He lived in the highest sky and no man ever saw him. His power was felt through lesser gods of the heavens—the Winds, the Sun, the Stars.

Symbol of Pawnee corn mother

At planting time, in a rite for the fertility of the earth, the Pawnees sacrificed an Indian girl captured from another tribe. She was said to represent Evening Star, patroness of growing plants in Pawnee mythology. Her soul went to her husband in the sky, Morning Star. He clothed her with the colors of the dawn and set her in the sky. Together they brought the renewal of vegetation on the earth. The Pawnees believed that if this sacrifice was not made, the crops would fail completely.

It is many years since this sacrifice has been performed. Without it the corn still grows.

The Pueblo Indians lived in the southwestern part of the United States, in New Mexico and Arizona. Many are still there. Pueblo country was part of a huge region with few rivers and little rain, almost a desert. Animals to hunt and wild plant food were both scarce. It was corn that kept the people alive, along with beans and squash. The Indians were sure that the corn was a gift of the gods. It was a beautiful gift; the ears of this corn grew in six colors: yellow, white, blue, red, black, and speckled. A perfect ear could be the emblem of a priest. Wrapped in feathers and jewels, it was placed on the altar at ceremonies, and it was carried by the dancing spirits of rain and fertility called *kachinas*. These spirits were present during half the year in the form of masked men, wearing bright paint and feathers, who danced the solemn Indian rituals. The kachinas were messengers between man and the gods.

The Hopis are Pueblo Indians living on mesas, flat-topped rocky hills, in northern Arizona. Many of the ancient ceremonies of the Hopis are still performed today, though there have been numerous changes.

The Hopi ceremonial year is a series of dramas picturing seedtime, growth, and harvest. It begins in December with Soyal, at the time of the winter solstice. During the sixteen days before this ceremony the Soyal priest and his assistants, but no one else, enter the *kiva,* an underground room used for religious ceremonies. There they make a sacred design in corn meal on the floor. This is their altar. Sacred ears of corn and other symbols are placed around the design; the walls of the kiva are decorated. All these things are messages to the spirits. Other messages are sent to the spirits at their own shrines, away from the kiva. These take the form of prayer sticks, lengths of wood with long feathers attached.

Seed corn is collected from the women of the village and blessed. After the ceremony it is returned to its owners, with promise of a plentiful harvest. The men are allowed to enter the kiva, and finally the women and children. They wait at night in the firelight of the kiva in breathless silence, with eyes fixed on the sacred design, praying that once again the sun will move its path upward in the sky and the days will grow longer.

A man dances about the kiva with great leaps. In some

villages he represents the god of vegetation. White dots painted all over his body symbolize the stars, and there is a huge star made of cornhusks on his head. He holds a painted buckskin shield fastened to a staff, edged with feathers to represent the sun. This he twirls wildly, to give the sun power for its summer journey.

Everyone goes home with prayer sticks and prayer feathers which are to be tied on rafters, on utensils, on dogs, on nearly anything. These will ensure that prayers to the spirits will continue without words in the months ahead.

In February the men who represent the kachinas go through the village bearing young bean plants as gifts for the children, along with dolls in kachina shape for the girls, bows for the boys. This is the Powamu ceremony, and it means that spring is on the way, because beans sprout in the spring. These particular beans have been secretly planted in the kivas where they were kept warm and watered, and songs were sung over them.

In the early spring a ceremony for the Great Serpent, bringer of fertility to both plants and people, takes place at night in the darkness of the kiva. At the beginning of the ceremony kachinas in costume sing and tramp about. Every now and then there is a great roar, said to be the voice of the serpent but really made by a gourd trumpet.

As the fire in the kiva blazes up the people can see, at one end of the kiva, a screen of cotton cloth painted with bright flowers and sun symbols. Before it stands a row of young corn plants which have been planted and tended in the same way as the beans. Huge heads of serpents, made of gourds, their big round eyes filled with seeds, poke through holes in the screen. Then the bodies of the serpents come wriggling out of the holes, to be blessed by the mother of the kachinas, impersonated as usual by a man. The bodies of the serpents are made of tubes of cotton cloth covering rings of willow. A man's arm inside this tube makes it move.

Finally, twisting about, the serpents knock over the row of young corn plants, thus acting out the harvesting of the crops.

When the ceremony is finished the room is darkened, the scenery is taken down, and the kachina actors go off to play their parts at another kiva. The miraculous corn plants are handed to spectators as a gift from the spirits. The people feel at peace, because once again their message, asking for increase of the crops, and of the people too, has found its way to the spirits.

At midsummer the kachinas leave the Hopi villages to return to their homes in the mountains. While they are there, for half the year, they are believed to visit the dead underground and hold ceremonies for them. No masked dances take place while the kachinas are gone. But before they leave, the "Home Kachina" dance, Niman, is held, at about the time of the summer solstice.

When this dance takes place the corn is beginning to ripen and other crops are growing well. Their bodies painted and glistening, the kachinas dance under the blazing sun and receive the thanks of the people. Every mark on kachina masks is full of meaning, every color and shape, every dot that carries the promise of corn or rain. These are spirit masks and the people look on them with awe and wonder.

The most famous of the Hopi ceremonies is the Snake

Ceremony, held every other year during the last days of August. Many visitors to Hopi country have witnessed this ceremony.

The Snake Ceremony asks the spirits for rain. Two secret societies, Antelope and Snake, are involved. First, priests of the Snake Society gather their relatives, the snakes, from all over the countryside. They take them to their kiva and wash them in a special ceremony, plunging them into a bowl of water and then tossing them onto a sacred sand painting. The priests sing all the while; they shake gourd rattles in rhythm. Antelope priests help the snake priests in this ritual.

On the last day of the ceremony, Antelope priests and Snake priests dance in the village plaza. Antelope priests dance first. Their bodies are painted in bright colors; around their necks hang shell and turquoise beads. They wear white kilts embroidered at the edge with designs of clouds and falling rain. Foxskins dangle at their backs with waving tails.

The Antelope priests circle the plaza, chanting all the while in a solemn rhythm. Then they line up to await the Snake priests. It is a tense and dramatic moment when the Snake priests enter the plaza. Spectators watch with breathless anticipation as the age-old drama is acted out.

The Snake priests move in the deliberate rhythm of a slow dance. Their faces are painted black, their bodies red. Like the Antelope priests, they wear necklaces and dangling foxskins. Their kilts are of red-brown deerskin, each one painted in back with part of the snake design. When the Snake priests line up side by side in the plaza, the design on the back of their kilts makes one continuous snake symbol. It is an impressive sight.

Then the Snake priests dance with the snakes. A priest

holds a snake in his mouth. Another priest behind him strokes the snake with a feather whip so it will stretch out and not coil or bite. All the time there is the rhythmic sound of chanting. Gourd rattles vibrate; they sound like rattle-snakes. The priests sway as they dance. The watching people feel the rhythm in themselves. Silently, they too sway with the dance.

At the end of the dance four priests pick up all the snakes and carry them off in the four directions—north, south, east, and west. There they release them. The snakes represent lightning and they will carry the message of the people to the spirits who send the rain.

Cloudbursts usually do follow the Snake Ceremony, and who can say that the ceremony has nothing to do with them?

There are dances at harvest, too; that is when the Hopi women have three special ceremonies of their own. Before the winter solstice old fires are put out and new ones made, with appropriate ceremony.

Then comes winter, and after that, not just in Hopi country but everywhere in the world, the eternal pattern of the year repeats itself—seedtime, growth, ripe fruit in the sunshine and the rain, and the good harvest. It is a pattern worth celebrating, surely a gift of the gods.

Epilogue

MANY THINGS HAVE CHANGED IN THE WORLD SINCE THE EARLY times with which this book began. On vast areas of land man grows his food in very different ways and, at the same time, his relationship to the earth beneath his feet has changed.

Long ago every family grew its own food. There was no other way. (Some of the food grown was for feeding animals that were also food for man.) In later times some farmers grew food for their families and for a number of other people besides, but still the majority of people were farmers. Almost everyone continued to live close to the land.

This is true even today in some parts of the world, especially in the poorer countries. Many of the farmers there grow only enough food for their own use. Others sell some of their rice or wheat or vegetables at nearby markets.

The use of machines on the land has changed farming completely in the more prosperous countries. There the farmer no longer breaks up the earth by pushing a plow through it by hand or by driving an animal that drags the plow. Instead, high-speed tractors pull sharp steel plows across the fields.

The farmer need not walk across his plowed land throwing handfuls of seed. A seed drill pulled by a tractor does the planting. The wheat farmer does not cut his ripe grain by hand with a sickle or a scythe. The job is done much faster by a harvesting machine. A few people can do work that used to require many, and as a result there are fewer farmers on the land.

All this is necessary. It would be impossible to feed the many people in the world today without the use of machines. In time every farm that is larger than a home garden may have machines to do the work.

The machines have brought other results, however. Much of the magic has gone out of growing food on the land. Some people seem to have no feeling about the land at all. Many have never dug their hands into the earth and felt of it, knowing that this is the living surface of the earth where, by processes that still seem miraculous, the plants grow that are food for the world.

We can get results without magic. We can grow food without rites to an earth mother, without praise to God at harvest. Springtime will follow winter, though we do nothing about it whatever.

But that is not the whole story. Something in us needs ritual, after all. The pattern of day and night, winter giving way to the blossoming world of spring, harvest of leaves that blow in the autumn wind—this is a ritual. It is a pattern not just in the natural world outside us, but deep within us, too.

Selected List of Books

OF SPECIAL INTEREST TO YOUNG PEOPLE

Dobler, Lavinia, *Customs and Holidays Around the World.* New York: Fleet Publishing Corporation, 1962.

Family Holidays Around the World (booklet). Washington, D.C.: American Home Economics Association, 1964.

Gaer, Joseph, *Holidays Around the World.* Boston: Little, Brown and Co., 1953.

Ickis, Marguerite, *The Book of Religious Holidays and Celebrations.* New York: Dodd, Mead and Co., 1966.

Sechrist, Elizabeth Hough, *Red Letter Days, a Book of Holiday Customs.* Philadelphia: Macrae Smith Co., 1965.

Some Latin American Festivals (booklet). Washington, D.C.: Pan American Union, 1956.

ADULT BOOKS

Bauer, Helen, and Carlquist, Sherwin, *Japanese Festivals.* New York: Doubleday and Co., 1965.

Burland, C. A., *The Gods of Mexico.* New York: G. P. Putnam's Sons, 1967.

Caso, Alfonso, *The Aztecs, People of the Sun.* Norman: University of Oklahoma Press, 1958.

Christian, Roy, *Old English Customs.* New York: Hastings House, 1966.

Elwin, Verrier, *The Religion of an Indian Tribe.* London: Oxford University Press, 1955.

Faron, L. C., *Hawks of the Sun.* Pittsburgh: University of Pittsburgh Press, 1964.

Frazer, Sir James George, *The New Golden Bough.* New York: S. G. Phillips, 1965.

Harper, Howard V., *Days and Customs of All Faiths.* New York: Fleet Publishing Corporation, 1957.

Hastings, James, ed., *Encyclopedia of Religion and Ethics.* New York: Charles Scribner's Sons, 1951.

James, Edwin O., *Seasonal Feasts and Festivals* (University Paperback). New York: Barnes and Noble, 1963.

——— *Comparative Religion* (University Paperback). New York: Barnes and Noble, 1961.

Kenyatta, Jomo, *Facing Mount Kenya*. New York: Random House (Vintage Books), n.d.

Linton, Ralph and Adelin, *We Gather Together, the Story of Thanksgiving*. New York: Henry Schuman, 1950.

McSpadden, Joseph Walker, *The Book of Holidays*. New York: Thomas Y. Crowell Co., 1958.

Osborne, Harold, *Indians of the Andes*. Cambridge: Harvard University Press, 1952.

Parrinder, Geoffrey, *African Traditional Religion*. London: Hutchison's University Library, 1954.

——— *West African Religion*. London: The Epworth Press, 1961.

Stein, William W., *Hualcan: Life in the Highlands of Peru*. Ithaca: Cornell University Press, 1961.

Underhill, Ruth M., *Red Man's Religion*. Chicago and London: University of Chicago Press, 1965.

Von Hagen, Victor W., *Realm of the Incas*. New York: The New American Library, 1957.

Watts, Alan W., *Easter, Its Story and Meaning*. New York: Henry Schuman, 1950.

Weiser, Francis X., *The Easter Book*. New York: Harcourt, Brace and Co., 1954.

Pronunciation List

Below are some of the words in the text which may be unfamiliar, with approximate English equivalents. Capitalized syllables are to be accented. Where two alternate pronunciations are given, either is acceptable. Words not on the list may be pronounced phonetically as spelled in the text. This includes Chinese words, the actual pronunciation of which cannot be accurately indicated in English equivalents.

Adonis	uh-DAHN-ihs
Allah	AH-luh
Allahabad	ah-luh-hah-BAHD
Antiochus	an-TIE-uh-kuhs
Aphrodite	af-ruh-DIE-tee
Artemis	ART-uh-mis
Arunta	uh-RUN-tuh
Asase Yaa	ah-SAH-say yah
Ashanti	uh-SHAN-tee
Attis	at-ihs
Aztec	AZ-tek
Bedouin	BED-o͝o-in
Beltane	BEL-tayn
Bhadon	BAH-dohn
Brahman	BRAH-muhn
Canaanite	KAY-nuh-night
Celt	selt, kelt
Ceres	SEER-eez
Cherokee	CHER-uh-kee
Cinteotle	seen-tay-OHT-l
Coatlicue	koh-aht-LEE-kway
Comus	KOH-muhs
Cuzco	KOOS-koh
Cybele	SIB-uh-lee
Demeter	dih-MEET-uhr
Dionysus	die-uh-NIE-sus
Diwali	dee-wah-lee
Ea	AY-ah
Eleusis	el-YOO-sis
fiesta	fee-ES-tuh
Floralia	floh-RAY-lee-uh
Gã	gah
Gaia	GAY-uh
Ganges	GAN-jeez
Gauri	gow-rih
gekonyi	geh-KAHN-yee
Hanukkah	HAH-no͝o-kah
Hanuman	HUN-o͝o-mahn
Hapi	HAH-pee
Holi	hoh-lee
Hopi	HOH-pee
Horus	HAWR-uhs
Hualcan	WAHL-kahn
Hunza	HUN-zah
Husain	ho͝o-SIGN
Inca	ING-kuh
Iran	ih-RAN
Iroquois	IR-uh-kwoy
Ishtar	ISH-tahr
Isis	EYE-sis
Islam	IS-lum, is-LAHM
kachina	kuh-CHEE-nuh
Kai	kigh
kami	kah-mee
Kenya	KEEN-yuh, KEN-yuh
Kikuyu	kih-KOO-yoo
kiva	KEE-vuh
Koran	koh-RAHN
Lakshmi	LUKSH-mee
Lucia	LOO-see-yuh

Maccabees	MAK-uh-beez
Makara Sankranti	MUH-kuh-ruh sahn-kran-tee
Mapuche	mah-POO-chay
Mardi Gras	MAHR-dee GRAH
Michoacan	MEE-choh-ah-kahn
Mir	meer
Mithras	MITH-ras
Moham-med	moh-HAM-id
Momus	MOH-muhs
Mwene Nyaga	mm-WAY-nay n-YAHG-gah
Natchez	NACH-iz
Ngai	n-GUY
No-ruz	noh-ROOZ
Nyame	NYAH-may
Odin	OH-din
Ome Tecuhtli	OH-may tay-COOT-lee
Osiris	oh-SIGH-ris
Pacha-mama	pah-kah-MAH-mah
Pakistan	PAK-ih-stan
Pawnee	paw-NEE
Pentecost	PEN-tuh-kawst
Persephone	puhr-SEF-uh-nee
Phagun	PAH-go͝on
Pharaoh	FAY-roh
Pluto	PLOO-toh
Powamu	POH-wah-mo͝o
Pueblo	PWEB-loh
Quechua	KECH-wah
Ra	rah
Rio de Janeiro	REE-oh day zhuh-NAYR-oh
Salii	SAL-ee-eye
Samhain	SAH-win
Saora	SA-o͝o-ruh
Saturnalia	sat-uhr-NAY-lee-uh
Shavuoth	shuh-VOO-uhs
Songgram	sohng-grahm
Soyal	sh͜oh-YAHL
Sukkoth	SOOK-uhs
Tammuz	TAH-mo͝oz
Tenoch-titlan	tay-nohch-tee-TLAHN
Thailand	TIE-luhnd
Thor	thawr
Tlaloc	tlah-LOHK
Tosi	toh-see
Totonac	toh-toh-NUK
Veracruz	ver-uh-KROOZ
Volador	voh-lah-DOR
Walpurgis	vahl-POOR-gis
Wassail	wah-SAYL
Xilonen	shee-LOH-nen
Xipe Totec	SHEE-pay toh-TEK
Xiuhte-cuhtli	shee-oo-tay-KOOT-lee
Yoruba	YOR-o͝o-buh
Zapotec	SAH-poh-tek
Zeus	zoos
Zuni	ZOO-nee

Index